D1594723

THE APPLE
OR
ARISTOTLE'S DEATH

(De Pomo sive De Morte Aristotilis)

MEDIAEVAL PHILOSOPHICAL TEXTS IN TRANSLATION

NO. 18

EDITORIAL BOARD

Marquette University Press
1131 W. Wisconsin Avenue
Milwaukee, Wisconsin

THE APPLE
OR
ARISTOTLE'S DEATH

(De Pomo sive De Morte Aristotilis)

Translated from the Latin

With an Introduction

by

Mary F. Rousseau, M.A.
Assistant Professor of Philosophy
Mount Mary College

MARQUETTE UNIVERSITY PRESS   MILWAUKEE, WISCONSIN
1968

Library of Congress Catalogue Card Number 68-28028

© Copyright, 1968, The Marquette University Press

Milwaukee, Wisconsin

Printed in the United States of America

To Edward,

who has taken the root
and delights in the fruit.

Acknowledgements

I wish to thank Panstwowe Wydawnictwo Naukowe, of Warsaw, for their permission to translate into English Marianus Plezia's Latin text of *Aristotelis qui ferebatur Liber de Pomo;* the Royal Asiatic Society of Great Britain and Ireland, for their permission to reprint Professor D. S. Margoliouth's English translation from Persian of *The Book of the Apple,* from the 1892 volume (n. s. XXIV) of the *Journal of the Royal Asiatic Society of Great Britain and Ireland;* and to the Cambridge University Press, for permission to quote from R. Hackforth's *Plato's Phaedo Translated with Introduction and Commentary* (Cambridge: University Press, 1955).

Table of Contents

Note on Abbreviations

The treatise under question in this study is one work, although it exists in several versions in various languages. Its earliest form is an Arabic version which became known to the modern world through a quite accurate Persian translation after the Arabic text itself was lost. A thirteenth century Hebrew version which purports to be a translation of the Arabic is so loosely done and so extensively modified from the original as to constitute a basically different, second version. The work is also referred to by several different, though similar, titles. In order to reduce this confusion, I shall refer to the work throughout my study by its simplest title: *The Apple*. Variants of this title will be noted when necessary. Statements about *The Apple* which do not specify any particular version are meant to apply to it generally, in all its known versions and translations.

The second, or Hebrew, version was soon translated into Latin and became enormously popular in medieval Europe. This Latin version, which closely follows the Hebrew and thus drastically departs from the Arabic original, is the chief focus of my study. But the other versions are also treated, though incidentally, as they illumine the Latin. Thus it is necessary to specify at times which version I am referring to. In order to simplify these references, I have devised the following abbreviations:

(1) A-P. This symbol refers to the Arabic-Persian version. The Persian translation has been published, whereas the recently discovered Arabic text has not. Thus the Persian text is at present our closest access to the original.

(2) H-L. This symbol refers to the second, the Hebrew-Latin version. In this study of medieval scholasticism, I am directing primary attention to the Latin translation of the Hebrew.

(3) One large part of my study is of the manuscript tradition of the Latin version. My work here is based on the catalogue of medieval Latin manuscripts of Aristotle, *Aristoteles Latinus*, assembled by Dulong, Franceschini, Lacombe, and Birkenmajer. The codices catalogued in *Aristoteles Latinus* are numbered consecutively throughout the three volumes. Thus I have found it convenient to refer to the Latin manuscripts of *The Apple* by their numbers in this catalogue. A typical citation will be *AL* 1774.

(4) The early printed versions of the Latin text are referred to by their numbers in *Gesamtkatalog Der Wiegendrucke*, thus: *GKW* 2450. For those which are available in American libraries, I also cite a number from Stillwell's *Incunabula and Americana 1450-1800*. An example of such citations is *A*860.

(5) Finally, I refer frequently to Moritz Steinschneider's catalog

[1]

of Hebrew translators, *Hebraeischen Übersetzungen.* The abbreviation for this title is *H.Ü.*

Table of Abbreviations

A-P: The Arabic-Persian version of *The Apple.*
H-L: The Hebrew-Latin version of *The Apple.*
A-L: *Aristoteles Latinus.*
GKW: *Gesamtkatalog Der Wiegendrucke.*
A: *Incunabula and Americana 1450-1800.*
H.Ü.: Hebraeischen Übersetfiungen.

Preface

The Apple, or Aristotle's Death is a purported death-bed dialogue, modelled on the *Phaedo,* in which the dying Aristotle discourses with his disciples on the supreme value of philosophy as the way to eternal salvation. The title comes from the apple whose life-sustaining fragrance is inhaled by Aristotle throughout the dialogue. This protreptic work, which exists in Arabic, Persian, Hebrew and Latin versions dating from the middle ages, is a patent attempt to first circumcise and then baptize Aristotle, that is to make him acceptable to Moslem and Hebrew thinkers and then to Christians. This task is attempted by having him repudiate his teachings on the eternity of the world and the mortality of the human soul. The dialogue began as a tenth century Arabic work, entering Europe by way of a Hebrew translation done by Abraham ben Chasdai at Barcelona in 1235; the Hebrew was then put into Latin by Manfred of Sicily in about 1255. From there it spread rapidly all over western Europe and, as I shall show, became a part of the Aristotelian corpus for the next three hundred years.

The work is thus a part of that vast and complex process, still imperfectly understood, by which the ideas and works of the ancient Greeks entered the intellectual life of western Europe—usually by way of Syriac, then Arabic, then Hebrew transmitters. While the ideas of the ancients were, to varying degrees, distorted by this process, and while their acceptance did decline rapidly after the peak of scholasticism in the thirteenth century, still, many of them have persisted and become a permanent and indispensable part of our intellectual heritage. One such idea—the wise man's contempt for the world—is a basic theme of *The Apple.*

Granted this context, it seems strange that a work which was vastly popular in both the Moslem and Christian worlds for several hundred years, which has been translated into half a dozen languages, which was included in the Aristotelian corpus by the schoolmen, and whose Latin version alone is now extant in almost a hundred manuscripts, should have received but scanty attention from historians of thought. Yet, such is the case of *The Apple.* Carra da Vaux, for example, makes no mention of it in his five volumes.[1] T. J. De Boer[2] refers only briefly to it, as does Brockelmann[3] in his vast history of Arabic literature. Nor is there any reference to it in the 1930 edition of

---

[1] Carra Da Vaux, *Les penseurs de l'Islam* (Paris: Librairie Paul Geuthner, 1921-26).

[2] T. J. De Boer, *The History of Philosophy in Islam* (London: Luzac and Co., Ltd., 1961 reprint of 1903 edition), pp. 24-25.

[3] C. Brockelmann, *Geschichte der Arabischen Litteratur. Erster supplementband* (Leiden: E. J. Brill, 1937), p. 373.

Nicholson's *Literary History of Arabs*.[4] Henri Corbin, in his recent history of Islamic philosophy, comments that the work was as popular among the Arabs as was the so-called *Theology of Aristotle* but gives little information about it in his two brief references.[5] A more recent two-volume, 1700-page *History of Muslim Philosophy*[6] has no indication in its extensive index of any reference to our dialogue. Nor have historians of western thought paid it much more attention. Thus, Geyer's volume of Ueberweg's *Grundriss*,[7] which treats of patristic and scholastic thought, does not refer to it; neither does Gilson in his *History of Christian Philosophy in the Middle Ages*.[8] Maurice de Wulf's three-volume history of medieval philosophy contains a single sentence about it, at the end of a paragraph on Manfred as a translator.[9]

Although relatively poor in both philosophic content and literary form, the dialogue is of some historical importance. First, by showing (as I shall demonstrate) that the Arabs of the tenth century had a direct knowledge of the *Phaedo,* it aids our understanding of what Raymond Klibansky has called the continuity of the Platonic tradition.[10] It is thus part of a large and growing set of facts which contradict the still common notion that the so-called Renaissance in western Europe was simply a return to the study of long-forgotten classical thought. The dialogue casts a great deal of light on the continuous transmission of Greek thought through Islamic and Hebrew intermediaries to the Christian west. It is, moreover, an interesting illustration of the fusion of ideas from widely separate cultures, because its basic theme is compatible with world-views as deeply different as those of Islam, Judaism, and Christianity. It is, then, an ecumenical document in a very basic sense. In fact, there is no immediately evident doctrinal indication of the religious persuasion of its author; he may have been pagan, Moslem, Jew, or Christian. The dialogue is also an illuminating instance of how a theme—philosophy and withdrawal from the world as the way to salvation—can persist intact while passing through different cultures. Finally, the treatise helps us to understand the puzzling demise of scholasticism which followed so hard upon a

---

[4] Published at Cambridge by the University Press in 1930.
[5] Henri Corbin, *Histoire de la philosophie islamique* (Paris: Gallimard, 1964), p. 36 and p. 198.
[6] Edited by M. M. Sharif (Wiesbaden: Otto Harrassowitz; vol. I, 1963; vol. II, 1966).
[7] Bernhard Geyer, *Die Patristische und Scholastische Philosophie* (Basel: Benno Schwabe und Co., 1951 reprint of 1928 edition). This is Vol. II of Friedrich Ueberweg, *Grundriss der Geschichte der Philosophie*.
[8] Published in New York by Random House in 1955.
[9] Maurice De Wulf, *Histoire de la philosophie médiévale*, vol. II (Paris: J. Vrin, 1947), p. 44.
[10] Raymond Klibansky, *The Continuity of the Platonic Tradition* (London: The Warburg Institute, 1939), p. 14.

promising beginning. The fact (which I shall demonstrate) that such a work could have been widely accepted as genuine by educated men shows the highly favorable attitude toward Aristotle which, while making scholasticism possible, also led in its exaggerated form to the collapse of the critical standards which had been achieved by, say, Thomas Aquinas in the thirteenth century. Thus our dialogue, while contributing little in a direct way to the development of philosophy, is a semi-precious document for the historian of thought. While *The Apple* is not itself an event in the history of thought, it illuminates for us the conditions which made possible other, truly historic events, such as the influx of Aristotle's *Metaphysics* and *De Anima* into Islam and the universities of Europe. In this sense it is worthy of study as a part of that process which is the history of human thought.

What research has been devoted to *The Apple* by modern scholars began in 1892, with D. S. Margoliouth's discovery and publication of a late (1630) Persian translation, to which he added a brief introduction and a translation into English.[11] The next year Steinschneider's catalogue of medieval Hebrew translators appeared, listing *The Apple* among pseudo-Aristotelian works and giving some information about its content and about the various translations, manuscripts, and printings of the Hebrew version.[12] A monograph about the dialogue, by Wilhelm Hertz, appeared posthumously in 1905, chiefly concerned to relate the work to other legends about Aristotle's death and about life-giving smells, particularly that of apples.[13] Hertz added some valuable information about the Latin version. The appearance in 1939 of the first volume of *Aristoteles Latinus,* the catalogue of the thousands of extant manuscripts of Aristotle, revealed that *The Apple* (or, in Latin, *Liber De Pomo sive de Morte Aristotilis*) was worth some careful attention, for that volume listed 37 manuscripts of it, scattered all over Europe; subsequent volumes of the catalogue were to list some 60 more.[14] A critical edition of the Latin version, with a quite informative introduction (also in Latin), was published by Marianus Plezia in the

[11] D. S. Margoliouth, "*The Book of the Apple* ascribed to Aristotle edited in Persian and English," in the *Journal of the Royal Asiatic Society of Great Britain and Ireland,* n.s. XXIV (1892), pp. 187-252. Margoliouth's translation is reprinted here (pp. 60-76) as an appendix

[12] Moritz Steinschneider, *Die Hebraeischen Übersetzungen des Mittelalters und die Juden als Dolmetscher* (Graz: Akademische Druck-U. Verlagsanstalt, 1956, p. 267). This is a reprint of the 1893 edition.

[13] Wilhelm Hertz, "Das Buch vom Apfel," in *Gesammelte Abhandlungen von Wilhelm Hertz,* ed. Friedrich von der Leyen (Stuttgart und Berlin: J. G. Cottas'che Buchhandlung Nachfolger, 1905), pp. 371-397.

[14] Georgius Lacombe, A. Birkenmajer, M. Dulong, and Aet. Franceschini, *Aristoteles Latinus* (*Pars Prior,* Paris: Desclée de Brouwer, 1939, reprinted 1957; *Pars Posterior,* Cantabrigiae: Typis Academiae, 1955; and *Supplementa Altera,* Paris: Desclée de Brouwer, 1961).

[5]

1954 volume of *Eos*, a Polish journal of philology. This text, with an expanded and updated introduction, was reprinted in 1960 as a separate fascicle in the series *Auctorum Graecorum et Latinorum*, at Warsaw.[15] Prior to Plezia's first edition, the Arabic version, which according to present knowledge is the original, had been unknown. But it was found in three manuscripts by the Orientalist Jörg Kraemer, who wrote an article about it—chiefly from the philological point of view—which appeared at Rome in 1956.[16] To my knowledge this Arabic text has not yet been edited.

We now find ourselves with some serious gaps in our knowledge of *The Apple*. Its origin—time, place, language of composition, and author—all remain unknown. While there is some evidence—which we shall examine later—that it began as a Greek work, the first certainty of its existence comes from a tenth century reference to the Arabic version, in the *Encyclopedia* of the Brothers of Purity at Baghdad. It was translated into Persian in the late middle ages,[17] and the Arabic was still being copied in the sixteenth century. But scarcely anything is known of this phase of its history. Somehow the treatise became available in Barcelona, where it was translated into Hebrew by Abraham ben Chasdai in 1235. This translation, which differs so drastically from the Arabic as to constitute another version of the work, found its way to Sicily, where Manfred put it into Latin in 1255; from there it found its way into universities all over Europe, from Italy to England, and from Poland to Spain. But few details of this history are known. Moreover, the content of the treatise, as well as its sources and subsequent influences, has never been studied from the point of view of the history of philosophy. Nor is there any translation from a critical text of the version which was so widely known to the schoolmen. Hardly any of the scattered sources of information about it, including

[15] Marianus Plezia, "Aristotelis qui ferebatur liber *De Pomo*. Versio latina vetusta interprete Manfredo duce," (*Eos*, 47, 1954), pp. 191-217. This text, with an updated introduction and notes in Latin, was reprinted separately under the title *Aristotelis qui ferebatur Liber De Pomo, Auctorum Graecorum et Latinorum Opuscula Selecta*, II (Varsoviae: Academia Scientiarum Polono, 1960). My references, unless otherwise noted, are to this second printing.

[16] Jörg Kraemer, "Das Arabische Original des pseudo-aristotelischen Liber De Pomo," in *Studi Orientalistici in onore di G. Levi della Vida* (Roma: 1956), pp. 486-506.

[17] One Persian manuscript dates from the thirteenth century; the translation was done by Afzallodin Kashani, a student of Nasiroddin Tusi (Cf. Corbin, *Histoire de la philosophie islamique*, p. 36). The manuscript which Margoliouth edited is from the seventeenth century; it is written in the margin of a version of the *De Anima* which was made in 1630 (Cf. H. Ethé, *Persian Manuscripts of the Bodleian Library*, p. 860). I have no information about the relations between these two manuscripts.

Plezia's excellent introduction, are in English. Hence this study and translation for the Marquette University series, *Medieval Philosophical Texts in Translation,* is offered.

I have no hope or intention of doing a definitive study which would answer these and other questions. Rather, I am offering an introduction, in the strict sense of the term, to the Latin version alone. This introduction will include a rudimentary doctrinal study, a synthesis and ordering of the historical information that is available, a survey of the Latin manuscript tradition, and an English translation of the Latin text. The definitive study of the work in all its versions awaits those with competence in the appropriate Oriental languages and the necessary vast knowledge of the currents of thought in the very sophisticated and complex intellectual life of medieval Islam and scholasticism. I am, however, happy that I can reprint as an appendix Professor Margoliouth's English translation of the Persian version. We shall thereby have some access, although indirect, to the Arabic original, which will enable us to illustrate some of the important differences between it and the Hebrew version from which our Latin work derives. Our only access to the Hebrew is also indirect, through the English translations by Kalisch and Gollancz.[18] But again, the doctrinal comparisons are so evident as to appear even in translation. And we have assurance that these translations are sufficiently accurate for this purpose.[19]

This translation and study of the Latin text are based upon the edition of Marianus Plezia, which is identical in its 1954 and 1960 printings. Plezia used seven of the ninety extant manuscripts, chiefly *AL* 1666 (*Cracoviensis, bibliotheca universitatis Jagellonicae* nr. 507), which is of thirteenth century Italian origin.[20] Plezia consulted eight

[18] Steinschneider, *loc. cit.,* lists the known manuscripts and printings of the Hebrew version. There are two modern English translations of the Hebrew, apparently independent of each other: Isidor Kalisch, *Ha-Tapuach: The Apple. A Treatise on the Immortality of the Soul by Aristotle the Stagyrite.* Translated from the Hebrew with Notes and Aphorisms. (New York: The American Hebrew, 1885) and Hermann Gollancz, *The Targum to "The Song of Songs"; The Book of the Apple; The Ten Jewish Martyrs; A Dialogue on Games of Chance.* Translated from the Hebrew and Aramaic (London: Luzac and Co., 1908). Both of these translations include brief notes but give us no significant information. I have used these two interchangeably, according to convenience. Both are readable; Gollancz's seems to be more scholarly, but neither is based on a modern critical text, which—as far as I could discern—does not exist.

[19] Cf. Kraemer, "Das Arabische Original," p. 486; Margoliouth, "The Book of the Apple," p. 188; Plezia, *Liber de Pomo,* pp. 18-19 for opinions on the accuracy of these various translations.

[20] The other manuscripts on which Plezia based his edition are: *AL* 640, *AL* 663, *AL* 725, *AL* 522, *AL* 1665, and *AL* 1842.

other manuscripts, three of the four known incunabula, and five editions of fragments which preceded his work.[21] I checked his text against photocopies of four manuscripts (*AL* 34, from the Pierpont Morgan Library in New York; *AL* 2050, from the Bodleian Library; and *AL* 2185 and 2186, both from the Vatican) and of one incunabulum (*GKW* 2341). Besides substantiating Plezia's text, these copies enabled me to correct and add to the information in *Aristoteles Latinus* about the content of the codices in which *The Apple* appears.

A summary of all the known versions and translations of our treatise seems in order here, even though some of them are tangent to our main purpose. *The Apple* began as a tenth-century Arabic work. It then passed into several distinct lines of translation:

(1) Into Persian (in about the seventeenth century) and thence into English (in the nineteenth). This English version—by Margoliouth—is reprinted below.

(2) Into a drastically modified Hebrew form (in the thirteenth century) and thence into Latin (in the same century). This medieval Latin version is the subject of the present study and translation into English.

(3) The Hebrew was put directly into English (by two recent translators, Kalisch in 1885 and Gollancz in 1908). I have made some slight use of these versions.

(4) The Hebrew was also translated into a corrupt, eighteenth century Latin version,[22] into German in the late nineteenth

[21] The manuscripts are *AL* 891, *AL* 890, *AL* 2096a, *AL* 2172, *AL* 2173, *AL* 2175, *AL* 2098, and *AL* 2035. The three incunabula, which I cite by their numbers in *Gesamtkatalog Der Wiegendrucke* (Leipzig: Karl W. Hiersemann, 1926), are *GKW* 2450, the *editio princeps* which appeared at Cologne in 1472; *GKW* 2341; *GKW* 2336. The other extant incunabulum, *GKW* 2451, is said by Kraemer ("Das Arabische Original," pp. 494-95) to accord with the *editio princeps*.

Lynn Thorndike in his article "The Latin Pseudo-Aristotle and Medieval Occult Science," in the *Journal of English and Germanic Philology*, XXI (1922), pp. 229-58, refers to an incunabulum at the British Museum as *IA. 49867*. Of the four editions mentioned above, three are to be found at the British Museum; since neither Thorndike nor *GKW* gives any further information, I cannot tell whether this is a fifth printing or one of the four I have already cited.

Two of the incunabula are available in American libraries. Cf. Margaret Bingham Stillwell, *Incunabula and Americana 1450-1800* (New York: Columbia University Press, 1930), numbers *A* 860 (*GKW* 2336) and *A* 865 (*GKW* 2341).

References to the sources of the fragments are in Plezia, *Liber De Pomo*, pp. 33-34.

[22] By J. J. Losius at Giesse in 1706. Margoliouth ("The Book of the Apple," p. 187), says that this translation is inaccurate and based on a corrupt text, and that the accompanying commentary is copious but irrelevant.

century,[23] and into Italian.[24] All of these translations are incidental to our present purpose.   ,

(5) The medieval Latin translation from the Hebrew has been recently put into Swedish[25] and—perhaps—Polish.[26]

The universal problem of translators—that of striking a balance between accuracy and readability—is compounded by the peculiarities of Manfred's style, especially in the prologue, which is of course his own composition. It is marked by repetition (the same word is sometimes used three or more times in the same sentence); by long, involved sentences (one sentence of the prologue consists of 109 words); and by long series of dependent clauses whose main verb and/or subject is only implied.

I have tried for literal accuracy first; but I have broken up some of the longer sentences, adjusted the punctuation and paragraphing to conform with English convention, used synonyms, and omitted some repetitions. Since the treatise attempts no technical precision of vocabulary, and since its chief value is literary rather than philosophical, I have in several places chosen readability over accuracy. It seemed pointless to reproduce exactly the flatness of the Latin; but enough of it remains so that the flavor of the Latin version will be obvious even to a casual reader.

I am happy to admit that my work could not have begun without the edition and the learned introduction of Marianus Plezia and the pioneer gathering of information by Wilhelm Hertz. In many cases my research consisted in furthering what they had begun by following leads suggested by them; where this is the case, I have indicated their work in the notes. Notes which cite Plezia and Hertz alone refer either to work which is original with them, or to information which they cite from sources that I could not obtain. Any failure to credit these and other scholars for their work is inadvertent, and I hope it will be pardoned. My own contributions are chiefly the translation, the comparison of *The Apple* to the *Phaedo,* and the survey of the Latin manuscript tradition.

23 By J. Musen at Lemberg in 1873. Cf. Steinschneider, *H. Ü.*, p. 268, and Margoliouth, *loc. cit.*

24 Cf. Steinschneider, *H. Ü.*, p. xxvii, citing Agost. Svetonio, *Il libro del miele et dell' anima per caver l'uomo dal fango* (in manuscript).

25 By Ingemar Düring in 1953, in *Florilegium Amicitiae, Festschrift E. Zilliacus,* pub. Helsingfors.

26 Plezia has a monograph, which I have not seen, entitled *Ps. Arystotelesowy Traktat De Pomo* (Sprawozdania . . . Polskiej Akademii Umiejetnosci LIII, 1952). This may be a translation of *The Apple* into Polish. Another of Plezia's works, "Neues zum pseudoaristotelischen *Buch vom Apfel,*" *Philologisches Vorträge,* 1959, pp. 191-96, summarizes the research to date without adding any information.

[9]

Special thanks must also go to Dr. John O. Riedl, who originally suggested the study and has been for several years the firm but gentle goad and helpful guide without whom it would never have come to be. Dr. Paul M. Byrne made many key suggestions and traced one incunabulum for me. The library staff at the University of Chicago provided willing and invaluable assistance. The grace and efficiency of the librarians of Marquette University were a constant surprise even to one who has been used to them for some years. Professor Richard Schneider of the University of San Francisco and Sister Louis Ellen of Alverno College gave help with some difficulties in the German sources. Professor Wadie Jwaideh of Indiana University very kindly translated the Arabic titles into English. Mrs. Alice Christensen typed the manuscript, and Mount Mary College gave financial aid. Sister Mary Eunice Silkey, S.S.N.D. and Gerald P. Caffrey assisted generously in the final proofreading. To all of these I give my thanks, and remind the reader that—like God in relation to His creatures—they are involved only in the good that I have accomplished. The remaining mistakes and deficiencies are all mine. I have not allowed these to keep me from publication because of the countervailing hope that others might correct them.

Finally, this little study is offered to my husband, Edward L. Rousseau. His sense of history has been my final cause; he also improved the translation in several places. May he find here a partial compensation for the loss of consortium he suffered while I was occupied with the pseudo-Aristotle.

Translator's Introduction

I. The Doctrinal Development of The Apple.

Nearly all modern scholars who know of *The Apple* point out its resemblance to the *Phaedo*, a resemblance which is obvious even from a casual reading of the work. Thus, Leopold Dukes, in a work on Ibn Gabirol, remarks that it imitates the *Phaedo* in being a death-bed discussion on immortality, but with Aristotle replacing Socrates as the main speaker.[1] Raymond Klibansky simply states the fact of the resemblance, without elaborating on it.[2] Jörg Kraemer saw evidence of some influence of Plato's *Phaedo* in the discussion of suicide which appears in all the known versions of *The Apple*. Contrary to Kraemer's suggestion that this influence was remote and indirect, however, perhaps through the writings of Clement of Alexandria and Theodoret,[3] internal evidence seems to indicate a closer and more immediate influence. In fact, it seems plausible to conclude that the author of the Arabic-Persian version had Plato's dialogue before him and with deliberate selectivity modelled his own work upon it. The story of the doctrinal development of this little work, then, must begin with a comparison between it and its Platonic exemplar. This resemblance is quite close in the Arabic version, which we shall examine first; it is diminished in the Hebrew-Latin.

The dialogue form, the death-bed setting, and the two disciples named Simmias and Kriton are the most obvious points of resemblance. Even the names of disciples which differ from those in the *Phaedo* are all Greek: Zeno, Stephanus, Kramas, Pindar, Eletus (or perhaps Theaetetus), Diogenes, and Lysias. The apple which gives our dialogue its title enters in by an ingenious adaptation of one of the incidents of the *Phaedo*: there Socrates, warned that conversation will generate body-heat that will interfere with the lethal drug that he is to take later in the day, dismisses the warning with the statement that the executioner can prepare a stronger dose.[4] In *The Apple* (A-P) Aristotle, too, is warned against talking lest the resultant body-heat interfere with a healing drug that has already been administered to him. He, too, dis-

---

[1] Leopold Dukes, *Salomo ben Gabirol aus Malaga und die ethischen Werke desselben* (Hannover, Telgener'schen Hofbuchdruck., 1860), p. 34. Cited by Steinschneider, *H. Ü.*, p. 267.

[2] Klibansky, *The Continuity of the Platonic Tradition*, p. 14.

[3] Kraemer, "Das Arabische Original," pp. 493-94. Both Clement and Theodoret transmit the passage on suicide from the *Phaedo*.

[4] 63D-E, p. 40. All references to and quotations from the *Phaedo* are from R. Hackforth, *Plato's Phaedo Translated with Introduction and Commentary* (Cambridge: University Press, 1955). I shall give both the Stephanus numbers and numbers of Hackforth's pages.

misses the warning, but explains that the only reason for prolonging life is the opportunity to converse. He then states that if the drug is thereby rendered ineffective, he will sustain his life by inhaling the fragrance of the apple which he holds in his hand.[5]

Another parallel between *The Apple* and the *Phaedo*, again not exact but close enough to indicate a deliberate selectivity, is in the disciples' reactions to their master's explanation of his confidence in the face of death. In both dialogues, the disciples accept the rational cogency of the main argument, and yet admit to a lingering fear of dying and ask for a further remedy. Socrates realistically refuses, explaining that such a change of attitude requires long effort on their own part and the help of many experts.[6] Aristotle, however, succeeds in converting his disciples from love of life to love of death,[7] and their

---

[5] Cf. below p. 60. References to the Arabic-Persian version are to Margoliouth's translation, reprinted below. Margoliouth noticed this point of resemblance to the *Phaedo;* cf. his "The Book of the Apple," p. 189.

Hertz traces a legend, which first appeared in the *Gesta Romanorum,* of a people who lived by smelling wild apples. He follows its reappearances, with variations, in Solinus, in Honorius Augustodensis, in Jakob of Vitry, Gervasius of Tilbury, Gautier of Metz, Rudolph of Ems, Thomas of Cantimpré, and, finally, John Mandeville. Cf. *Gesammelte Abhandlungen,* pp. 392-95.

The sacralization of the apple as the source of life appears in the cosmogonies of all the world's great religions, and in folk-lore and medicine of people widely separated in time and space. It has a very ancient origin, perhaps in neolithic initiation rites. Cf. Peter Gordon, *L'Image du monde dans l'antiquité* (Paris: Presses Universitaires de France, 1949), pp. 83-97.

The apple which Aristotle sniffs has perhaps its closest parallel in a sacred drama of the Persians which portrays the death of Mohammed; at his last moment, the Prophet inhales the fragrance of an apple, brought by an angel, which endows him with eternal life. Cf. Gordon, *L'Image du monde,* p. 92, cited by Plezia, *Liber de Pomo,* p. 66.

The Jews have a similar tradition. The Hebrew word for *apple* (*tappuah*) is derived from the root meaning "sweet-scented," and there are several references in the Bible itself and in Hebrew biblical tradition to the use of the scent of apples to revive the sick. The most famous of these is, of course, from the Canticle of Canticles, "Comfort me with apples, for I am sick of love" (2, 5).

Linguists and botanists disagree about the translation of the term: the Greek (*melon*) and Latin (*malum*) equivalents were used to refer to several similar fruits (e.g. pomegranite and quince) as well as the apple itself. The Arabic word for apple (*tuffah*) is probably from the Syriac name for a fruit which was not as tasty as our apple, but was prized for its fragrance and used to revive the sick or the faint. In rabbinical literature the apple came to symbolize the divine beauty, which was said to diffuse itself into the world like an apple. Cf. "Apple." *The Jewish Encyclopedia,* vol. II (New York: Ktav Publishing House, Inc., 1901), pp. 23-24.

[6] 77A-78B, pp. 77-79.

[7] See below, Margoliouth's translation, Appendix, pp. 62-63. All quotations from *The Apple* (A-P) are from this appendix.

conversion then becomes an occasion for a discussion of suicide which closely resembles that in the *Phaedo*. Socrates there flatly denies that the philosopher's longing for death could ever justify his putting an end to himself, because we are the property of the gods, whose sole right it is to determine the length of our days in the body.[8] In *The Apple*, suicide is also rejected, on the grounds that the soul is in the body under the orders of a superior, like a guardian stationed at a pass who—while looking forward to the glory of ultimate victory—does not violate his orders.[9] The reason for the rejection of suicide may, in fact, be identical in both dialogues, for the term which Socrates uses in the *Phaedo* to express figuratively the relation between soul and body is ambiguous, meaning that the soul is either the guardian of the body or its prisoner.[10]

Furthermore, the actual death-scene of *The Apple* shows a similarity with differences which indicates a conscious use of the *Phaedo*. In the Platonic dialogue, the disciple most intimately involved in Socrates' death is Crito, to whom the philosopher speaks his last words, and who closes the eyes and mouth of the corpse. The dialogue ends with the famous eulogy in which Phaedo calls Socrates the wisest man of his generation.[11] Aristotle, in *The Apple*, turns to Kriton in his last moment, taking that disciple's hand and laying it on his face. He speaks a final prayer, drops the apple, and dies. This dialogue also closes with an exclamation of the philosopher's greatness, one which by implication makes its hero the wisest man not only of his generation, but of all time: "The day of knowledge is over."[12]

An analysis of the doctrine of the two dialogues also indicates a carefully selective use of the *Phaedo* by our author. The moral theme of the *Phaedo* has been adopted intact: the flight from bodily pleasures and the pursuit of wisdom effect a purification which leads to salvation after death. The true philosopher, consequently, welcomes death as

---

[8] 61D-62C, pp. 35-36.
[9] Appendix, p. 63.
[10] The word is *phroura*. The view of the soul as the guardian of the body was favored by Cicero and the Stoics; Burnet, however, favors the other interpretation on grounds of linguistic analysis. Cf. Burnet's note on *Phaedo* 62B in John Burnet, *Plato's Phaedo edited with Introduction and Notes* (Oxford: The Clarendon Press, 1911), pp. 22-23. Erasmus preferred the guardian-figure; in "The Godly Feast," Nephalius is made to say: No less choice is the speech of

Socrates in Plato: 'The human soul is placed in this body as if in a garrison which it must not abandon except by the commander's order'. . . . The more significant that Plato said "garrison" instead of "house," since . . . . in a garrison we are assigned some duty by our commander. Cf. Craig R. Thompson (trans.) *The Colloquies of Erasmus* (Chicago: The University of Chicago Press, 1965), p. 67.
[11] 118A, p. 190.
[12] Appendix, p. 76.

the fulfillment of his life-long striving. The over-all rhythm of this theme as it is stated, reiterated, forgotten in the discussion of related issues, returned to after digressions, and restated at the end is parallel in the two works. The very structure in which the theme is first presented is also the same: in both dialogues, the speakers are first made to agree on the excellence of wisdom. The master then poses alternatives: this excellence is to be achieved either in this life or in the next. The first alternative is then ruled out, on the basis of common experience, and the conclusion is that the fullness of knowledge is attained only after death. The corollary is that a fear of dying shows a man to be not a true philosopher but, rather, a fool: he has deprived himself of the pleasures which would make this life worth living and yet shrinks from the far greater pleasure of the next life which had been his object all along.[13] In fact, several of these passages seem so similar that a close textual study might reveal them to be verbatim quotations. For example, in requesting an explanation from Socrates for his joy at imminent death, Plato's Simmias says,

> Do you propose to keep these ideas to yourself, or will you let us share in them before you leave us? I really think this is a blessing in which we have a right to share: and moreover if you can persuade us of what you say, that defence you spoke of will be achieved.[14]

The Simmias of *The Apple* says,

> If you have this confidence, it were better that you should explain the ground of it to us also, that we may be as certain as you.[15]

Again, the agreed upon definition of death is the same. In the *Phaedo*, Socrates says,

> And by death do we not mean simply the departure of soul from body? Being dead consists, does it not, in the body having parted from the soul and come to be by itself, and in the soul having been parted from the body, and being by itself.[16]

In *The Apple,* we read,

> Death, horrible as it is to the vulgar, is nevertheless nothing but the freeing of the soul from its bodily case?[17]

And again, "Death is nothing else but the soul surviving the body."[18]

Assertions that the body is detrimental to the philosopher's search for wisdom are also similar in the two dialogues. Socrates puts it thus:

---

[13] Cf. *Phaedo,* 62C-69E, pp. 39-56 and Appendix, below, p. 64.
[14] 63B-D, p. 40.
[15] Appendix, p. 60.

[16] 64C, p. 44.
[17] Appendix, *ibid.*
[18] *Ibid.,* p. 71.

The clearest knowledge will surely be attained by one who
. . . gets rid, so far as possible, of eyes and ears and, broadly
speaking, of the body altogether, knowing that when the body
is the soul's partner it confuses the soul and prevents it from
coming to possess truth and intelligence.[19]

Aristotle similarly says,

Do you not see that the desires and delights of the body
. . . impede the search after wisdom? . . . Then, since you confess that lusts have the power to damage the intellect, surely the
body which enjoys those lusts must be more detrimental to the
intellect?[20]

In regard to the philosopher's freedom from the fear of dying,
Socrates speaks thus:

. . . it would be ridiculous that a man should spend his life
in a way that brought him as near as possible to being dead,
and then complain of death when it came. . . . How unreason-
able not to be glad to go to a place where they may hope to
get what they have longed for all their lives, to wit intelligence,
and to be rid of the presence of their old enemy![21]

Aristotle expresses the idea in like phrases:

For he who weans his soul from pleasures and undertakes
the labour of searching for wisdom for the sake of God, and to
gain the reward therefor after death, if at the hour of death he
exhibits melancholy, makes himself an object of laughter and
derision.[22]

And both dialogues speak in like terms of the fear of dying as
a sign that a man has not become a true philosopher. Socrates says,

Then if you see a man about to die complaining, is not that
good evidence that he is not really a philosopher, a lover of
wisdom, but what we may call a lover of the body? And
probably he will be a lover of riches too, or of honours, or
maybe of both.[23]

Aristotle's words on this topic are:

If ye abstain in this world from lusts, but are attached to this
world in your heart, your abstinence is not perfect. Now the
root of attachment to the world lies in love of self-preservation.
Hence everyone who abstains from its lusts, but desires to
remain in the world has caught the branch and neglected the
root.[24]

As a further evidence of imitation of the *Phaedo* in this discussion of
the philosopher's attitude toward death, the author of *The Apple* ex-

[19] 65E-66A, p. 47.
[20] Appendix, p. 61.
[21] 67E-68A, p. 53.

[22] Appendix, p. 64.
[23] 68C, p. 54.
[24] Appendix, p. 62.

plicitly attributes his disjunctive method of argumentation to Socrates.[25]

The doctrine which contrasts true and false virtue is also fundamentally the same in these two dialogues. Socrates in the *Phaedo* attributes to ordinary men a false temperance, which exchanges lesser pleasures for greater ones, and a false courage, which accepts lesser fears in order to avoid greater ones. The philosopher, on the other hand, is said to practice true virtue, which is the renunciation of all pleasures and fears for the sake of wisdom.[26] Similarly, Aristotle in *The Apple* accuses ordinary men of fraudulent and wasted mercy, veracity, and liberality, which lead their possessors to unfitting and self-seeking actions that are vicious rather than virtuous. True virtue is said to be that which is vivified by wisdom.[27]

Here again, the verbal similarities between the two dialogues seem close even in translation. In the *Phaedo,* Socrates' words are:

> . . . True virtue in general is that which is accompanied by intelligence, no matter whether pleasures and fears and all the rest of such things be added or subtracted. But to keep these apart from intelligence and merely exchange them for each other results, I fear, in a sort of illusory façade of virtue, veritably fit for slaves, destitute of all sound substance and truth.[28]

The Aristotle of *The Apple* says:

> The vulgar herd have a sort of knowledge and science and truth and honesty and generosity and other wasted virtues which are as different from wisdom as the form of an animal is from a picture or sketch on a wall.
>
> Diogenes: Why do you call those virtues of the vulgar herd *wasted?*
>
> Aristotle: On account of the ignorance of the vulgar with regard to them. . . . The knowledge of the wise man vivifies his actions, whereas the folly of the ignorant mortifies his.
>
> Diogenes: Then are their good actions any better than their bad ones or not?
>
> Aristotle: They are not.[29]

Last of all, *The Apple* explicitly attributes to Plato a doctrine which appears in the *Phaedo,* though without mentioning the dialogue by title. A disciple asks for an explanation of the Platonic dictum that a philosopher ought to accumulate vast quantities of things that both do good and avert evil, while seeking only small amounts of those which avert evil without doing any positive good. Aristotle interprets

---

[25] *Ibid.*, p. 70.
[26] 67E-69E, pp. 53-56.
[27] Appendix, pp. 74-75.

[28] 69B-C, p. 55.
[29] Appendix, *ibid.*

this teaching to mean that the philosopher ought to seek a plenitude of one thing only—knowledge. The means of subsistence he should seek only to the minimum degree necessary, while all other things— even an excess of the means of subsistence—are to be avoided as doing positive evil. While this interpretation is based directly on the specialized metaphysics of *The Apple*, which categorizes good and evil as knowledge and ignorance, respectively, it does accurately reflect Socrates' teaching in the *Phaedo*.[30]

The most striking doctrinal difference between the two works is that in the *Phaedo*, the moral suasion is given a solid metaphysical and epistemological foundation. The soul's immortality is rooted in its knowledge of and resemblance to the Forms, and the ultimate reason for shunning bodily pleasure is that it effects an attachment to visible things that distorts our judgment about what is really real.[31] None of this appears in *The Apple*—neither the Forms, nor recollection, nor skepticism about sense-perception. Nor is there any questioning of the fact of immortality. The rejection of bodily pleasures rests only on an implicit and unexplained dualism which opposes matter to spirit; wisdom is said to require the diminution of bodily humors, whereas indulgence in pleasure increases them. Death, of course, is their complete abatement and thus the soul's release.[32] The sketchy metaphysics of *The Apple*, neither clearly defined nor completely developed, reduces all things—human actions, natural things, etc.—to the categories of "knowledge, ignorance, and the recompense of the two."[33] But even here we can detect the literary, if not philosophical, influence of the *Phaedo*. As in Socrates' discussion of immortality, Aristotle's categorization of things as either knowledge or ignorance takes the form of a genuine dialogue in which ideas are progressively, sometimes dramatically, clarified and arguments are advanced by the give-and-take of objection and reply between the master and his disciples and, occasionally, among the disciples themselves. In fact, in both dialogues a point is reached at which the disciples raise such forceful objections as to threaten to reduce themselves to complete confusion and doubt.[34] They then call on their master for rescue, and in both cases he provides it, by means of an appeal to religious belief. Socrates, thus, confirms his arguments for immortality by asserting the soul's resemblance to the gods,[35] while Aristotle appeals to a saying of Hermes, said to be quoted in his own *Physics*, which finally convinces his disciples

[30] Cf. *Phaedo*, 64D-67B, pp. 45-48 and the appendix below, pp. 73-74.
[31] 82D-84A, pp. 92-94.
[32] Appendix, p. 61.
[33] *Ibid.*, pp. 70-71 and 73-74.
[34] Cf. *Phaedo*, 88C-89A, pp. 100-106 and the appendix below, pp. 69-72.
[35] 106D-E, p. 160.

that all the things of this world ought to be abandoned because they are in the category of ignorance.[36]

The marvelous story in the *Phaedo*[37] in which Socrates distinguishes the different classes of men and elaborately describes their respective fates after death has no close parallel in *The Apple*. The wise-just-truthful are contrasted with the foolish-unjust-mendacious as good and evil, respectively, but our author makes no attempt to discern implications for life after death.[38] Nor is there anything comparable to Socrates' intellectual autobiography, which implicitly exemplifies for his disciples the method for the pursuit of wisdom. Instead, Aristotle's disciples request and receive explicit instruction in how to learn philosophy—what topics to pursue, in what order, and which books to consult after their master is dead. Aristotle recommends that, since wisdom is a characteristic of the soul rather than of the body, one should begin with the study of his own soul. Such study, however, requires the aid of a teacher. In an ingenious fusion of the ancient theory of vision with the Socratic maieutic, he explains that just as the eye is the source of vision and yet needs to converge with an external light in order to see, so is the soul the source of wisdom which yet needs to encounter the higher wisdom of a teacher in order to understand.[39] By implication the study of anything other than the soul is said to be an impediment to wisdom.

As sources to consult in the event of disagreement, Aristotle recommends the following: the book of Hermes, The *Politics*, the *Physics*, the *Ethics*, and the four books of Logic, namely, the *Categories*, *Peri Hermeneias*, *Analytike*, and *Apodeiktike* or book of *Demonstration*.[40]

---

[36] Appendix, pp. 72-73.

[37] 80E-82A, pp. 87-90 and 107C-115A, pp. 167-84.

[38] Appendix, pp.67-69 and p. 74.

[39] *Ibid.*, p. 75. This is apparently the passage which Margoliouth used, prior to Kraemer's discovery of the Arabic text, to authenticate the Persian translation. He rightly saw that the passage, which appears as a fragment (written in Hebrew characters) in the anonymous *Risalat al-Burhan fi tadkiyat al-hayawan* (*Epistle of Demonstration Concerning the Rousing of Animals*), fol. 19ᵛ of Bolleian Codex *Hunt.* 345, corresponds exactly with a passage in the Persian version, whereas there is nothing resembling it in the Hebrew. Cf.

Margoliouth, "The Book of the Apple," pp. 187-191.

My identification of this passage rests on Kraemer's statement ("Das Arabische Originale," p. 491) that the fragment deals with Aristotle's doctrine on *nous* and on his optics.

Though both Margoliouth and Kraemer cite Steinschneider's catalogue for information about the manuscript in which this Arabic fragment occurs, they give different dates for it. Margoliouth, referring to p. 674 of *Catalogus Bibl. Hebr. quae in Biblioth. Bodleiana asservantur*, assigns it to the thirteenth century. Kraemer, citing p. 675 of the same work, assigns it to the twelfth.

[40] Appendix, p. 76.

[18]

This is an interesting list not only for the information it gives about the transmission of Aristotle's works to the Islamic world, but also for the substitution of the book of Hermes for the *Metaphysics*. We may suppose, since all the other titles are here correlated with their correct contents, that the substitution was deliberate—a feature which lends credence to Margoliouth's speculation of Sabaean authorship for *The Apple*.[41] Aristotle's description of the supernatural origin of philosophy is also consonant with Sabaean tenets: It is said to have come as a revelation from God to the Archangels, and thence to Hermes; he in turn transmitted it to the "heralds and ambassadors of the different response to the call of the "heralds and ambassadors of the different ages in the different regions of the globe," then taught it to mankind.[42]

In summary, we can conclude that while the author of *The Apple* does not mention the *Phaedo*, he had that Platonic dialogue before him as a model. Evidence for this conclusion is found in the structure and the doctrine of the dialogue. The setting, the form, and the names of two of the characters are direct borrowings. The moral theme and the pattern of its argumentation are also parallel. Patterns of argumentation are the same even where content differs. The subordinate issues of suicide and of genuine versus spurious virtue are similarly discussed in both works. And finally, *The Apple* makes two specific and accurate references, once naming Socrates and once Plato, to doctrines found in the *Phaedo*.

This influence of the *Phaedo* helps us, then, to understand the complex process by which Plato's works were transmitted through the Arabs of the middle ages to the Christian west. Klibansky does not mention the *Phaedo* in his list of Platonic dialogues which were known to the Arabs in the ninth century; but certainly we have evidence here that it was known in the tenth. The Arabic version of *The Apple*, as we shall see later, may have been translated from an earlier Greek version, perhaps—as is the case with many Greek philosophic works— by way of a Syriac intermediary. At any rate, if it is as close to the *Phaedo* as it appears to me to be, publication of an edition of the recently discovered Arabic text of *The Apple*, as part of the *Plato Arabus* project, would seem to be warranted. As outlined by Klibansky, *The Apple*, would come under the heading of "Arabic Writings on and Paraphrases of Plato's Works," rather than under his "Arabic Recasting

[41] Cf. Margoliouth, "The Book of the Apple," p. 190, where he mentions that the pseudo-Sabaeans of Harran, who claimed Hermes as their founder, provided many prominent translators of Greek philosophical works. Since they were star-worshippers, the interpolated attack on this form of idolatry in the Hebrew version may well have been inspired by knowledge of, or speculation about, such authorship. See below, pp. 54-56.

[42] Appendix, p. 75.

of Neoplatonic Works," for it is an instance of direct influence from the *Phaedo* itself.[43]

While an Arabic translation of the *Phaedo* has never been traced, quotations fro mit (in Arabic) are in a work on India by Al-beruni, a Persian linguist and geographer who lived c.973-c.1048. He used a version which lacked the dialogue form, however.[44] Our author knew —and imitated—that structure.

Our Arabic author's use of the *Phaedo* was, however, selective. His aim was a moral one—to persuade men to the philosophic life as the way to salvation. Unwilling to accept the metaphysics and epistemology of the *Phaedo*, he omitted all references to the Forms and to recollection. He likewise omitted the arguments for immortality which depend on these doctrines and had all his interlocutors—despite their Greek names—take the fact of an afterlife for granted.

The substitution of Aristotle for Socrates may be explained as a deliberate attempt to make the Stagyrite the fount of all wisdom. If our author was a Moslem or a Christian, it may have been an attempt to make Aristotle more acceptable to believers, for the vagueness of

[43] Cf. Klibansky, *The Continuity of the Platonic Tradition*, p. 14 and p. 53.

[44] Cf. the English translation by E. Sachau (*Alberuni's India*, London: Kegan Paul, Ltd., 1910), vol. II, p. 288. If it is true, as Richard Walzer states in his "Arabic Transmission of Greek Thought to Medieval Europe," *Bulletin of the John Rylands Library*, no. 1 (July, 1945, pp. 160-183), that by the tenth century the Arabic translators knew no Greek and worked exclusively from Syriac translations, it would seem that a Syriac version of the *Phaedo* was available as a model for the Arabic author of *The Apple*. It is also possible, of course, that our Arabic version is a translation from an earlier Syriac or Greek composition. See my introduction, pp. 28-29, below.

Walzer's article on Plato in the new edition of the *Encyclopedia of Islam* summarizes recent knowledge about the access of the Arabs to Plato's dialogues. (R. Walzer, "Aflatun," *Encyclopedia of Islam*, ed. H. A. R. Gibb *et al.*, London: Luzac Co., 1960, pp. 230-235). Although the Arabic bibliographers mention the titles of all the Platonic dialogues, no manuscript of an Arabic translation of any one of them has been traced. In addition to Alberuni's quotations from the *Phaedo*, Walzer says that a Persian version of that dialogue is in Brusa; but he gives no information about it. He also refers to the long-known fact that the death-scene of the *Phaedo* is reproduced by both al-Qifti and ibn Oseiba, Arabic biographers of the thirteenth century. Steinschneider points out (*H.Ü.* p. xvii) that the names of three of Socrates' disciples in both of these versions of his death are the same as three of the disciples in *The Apple*—an indication of influence from our dialogue. I was not able to examine these two descriptions of Socrates' death—they may even be from *The Apple* rather than the *Phaedo*; the scribes who copied the Arabic text of *The Apple* substitute Socrates for Aristotle in two of the three known manuscripts, a practice which could have had its origin as early as the thirteenth century. See my introduction, below, pp. 32-33.

[20]

his genuine doctrine on the afterlife was one point on which his philosophy found serious resistance among People of the Book. Thus, to attribute to him the sentiments expressed in this work would be a strategic move. On the other hand, our author may have been simply victimized by the error, ancient in origin, which attributed Platonic and neo-Platonic doctrine to the Stagyrite.[45]

The Apple (A-P) is much poorer in philosophical content than Plato's masterpiece; it is in fact a work of rhetoric rather than of demonstration. And yet, it is not to be scorned, even on literary grounds. While the author was no Plato, he did have a rare ability to recognize and re-create the psychological drama of the great philosophical issues of life and death, of virtue and vice, and of the nature and value of philosophy itself.

If *The Apple* (A-P) is inferior in both style and content to its Platonic model, the relative poverty of its Hebrew-Latin version, *De Pomo*, is even more striking. In fact, the unavoidable impression is that the Hebrew translator, finding to hand what he thought was an Aristotelian work expressing an important moral doctrine, used it as a distant model for a new composition. In this new work, he adopted the principal theme and some of the related topics of discussion, but added notions that were by his time part of the common store of western philosophers, and made interpolations designed to magnify the authority of Aristotle. All of this he cast into a rough approximation of the original dialogue form, but with no attempt to reproduce the conversation exactly, to follow accurately the line of argumentation, or to preserve either the psychological drama or the literary elegance of his model.[46]

The translation from Arabic to Hebrew was done at Barcelona in 1235 by rabbi Abraham bar Chasdai.[47] It is directed at certain "weaklings among our people" who would destroy belief in a life after

---

[45] This error appears in al-Kindi's compilation of the so-called *Theology of Aristotle*, which consists in fact of extracts from Plotinus. The confusion is compounded by the prologue, which makes Porphyry a disciple of Aristotle. Cf. Paul Henry et Hans-Rudolph Schwyzer (eds.), *Plotini Opera*, Tomus III, Mvsevm Lessianvm Series Philosoph. XXXIV (Paris: Desclée de Brouwer et Cie., 1959), p. 486, note 1.

[46] This next comparison is a development

of Plezia's suggestion in his article, "Neues zum pseudoaristotelischen *Buch vom Apfel*."

[47] Plezia, *Liber De Pomo*, p. 20. The known manuscripts and printed editions of this Hebrew version are listed in Steinschneider's *Hebraeischen Übersetzungen*, pp. 267-270. Margoliouth adds to these a 1799 edition with commentary which appeared at Grodno under the name of J. Lichstein ("The Book of the Apple," p. 188).

[21]

death.[48] Margoliouth's judgment that "the Hebrew translation is a very unfaithful abridgment in which the original purpose of *The Book of the Apple* is entirely obscured,"[49] is, however, a bit too harsh. The moral purpose of exhortation to the philosophic life as the way to salvation persists and is, in fact, strengthened: Abraham is called the Philosopher, and the science of philosophy is declared a divine mode of knowledge.[50] Moreover, the setting—including the life-giving apple—is retained; Aristotle remains the hero; and the names Simo and Crito are apparent translations of Simmias and Kriton.

The work is much shortened, however, with the number of speakers (apart from one or more who are unnamed) reduced from ten to five; Melon (also called Melion and Meliton in the Latin) and Aristoros (Arastaratus in the Latin) appear in addition to Aristotle, Simo, and Crito. While there is some vestige of the dialogue form, *The Apple* (H-L) is in fact a series of lengthy monologues by Aristotle, interrupted by brief interjections from the disciples and by one long speech by Melon.

The opening paragraph is new: a group of wise men, frustrated in their search for the right way to live, are said to have assembled and determined that the only path of rectitude is love of neighbor, avoidance of evil, confession of the truth, self-judgment, and fear of the

---

[48] So says the translator in his prologue. Cf. Hermann Gollancz, *The Targum to 'The Song of Songs'; The Book of the Apple; The Ten Jewish Martyrs; A Dialogue on Games of Chance. Translated from the Hebrew and Aramaic* (London: Luzac and Co., 1908), pp. 91-92. Chasdai's entire prologue is worth quoting here:

Abraham the Levite, Bar-Chisdai, says: When I reflected upon this book and its contents, composed by the sages of Greece, I thought that it might be of service in the interests of our Faith to strengthen the hands of the weaklings among our people. By weaklings I mean those who meditate upon the words of the heretics, who aver that, after the dissolution of the body, man has no real existence, and that man lives solely by reason of bodily existence, whereas, at his death, nothing remains. Such adduce, as a proof of their statements, the various exist-

ing substances which have a value by means of their combination. Take for example, the ingredients of ink with which we write: through the combination of the various medicaments, we get a real substance, the result of which is a black liquid of use for writing, whereas each ingredient taken apart would not serve the purpose. The same may be said of the ingredients of dyestuffs and other objects. Such heretics apply all their energies to the task of destroying faith: and it is to these that Scripture refers when it says, "And they shall be an abhorring to all flesh" (Isaiah lxvi. 24).

It is for this reason that I have determined to translate this book from Arabic into Hebrew: and I now commence. (Gollancz, pp. 91-92).

[49] "The Book of the Apple," p. 188.
[50] Gollancz, *The Targum to 'The Song of Songs'* etc., p. 98, p. 108, and p. 114.

Creator.[51] Their sorrowful meeting at Aristotle's death-bed and their request for an explanation of his cheerful spirits are repeated from the Arabic version. However, Aristotle explains his sniffing of the apple by the mere fact that the sensitive soul is strengthened by good odors; the dramatic emphasis on the value of philosophic conversation which appeared in *The Apple* (A-P) is thus lost.[52]

The next section is an interpolation describing health, sickness, and death in terms of the equilibrium among the four contraries—hot and cold, dry and moist.[53] The following passage describing the four souls in man is also an innovation.[54]

As in the Arabic work, Simo (Symas) then asks the master to explain his confidence in the face of death and to free his disciples from their own fear of dying. His response is substantially the same as in the Arabic work, namely that philosophy, which is the most excellent of things, finds its fulfillment either in the next life or not at all. The Hebrew translator, however, adds two aspects which strengthen this argument: one, that philosophy is the mark which distinguishes man from the beasts, and thus to deny its value is to reduce man to the status of a beast; the other, a reference to the problem of evil, that an afterlife is needed to rectify the inequities of this life, which so often sees the wicked prosper while those who truly pursue wisdom suffer.[55]

One of the points Aristotle makes here contradicts the Arabic-Persian version. He recommends that one who finds the direct understanding of his own soul and of God too difficult might begin by a study of his body, in whose subtle structure he might discern a reflection of the wisdom of the Creator.[56] Such a procedure is rejected outright in the Arabic work, where all material things are seen as impediments to true wisdom, whose only source is the interior of one's own soul.

The next discourse, whose point is that the true philosopher welcomes death as his soul's final release from all impediments to wisdom, also parallels the Arabic version, but as a précis rather than a verbatim translation. The bodily humors are named and described in more detail, and the content of philosophy is presented more precisely: philosophy

---

[51] See my translation, below, p. 50. Since the Latin corresponds closely to the Hebrew, with a few exceptions references will be to my translation of the Latin. Exceptions will be noted as they occur.
[52] *Ibid.*
[53] See below, pp. 50-51.
[54] See below, p. 51. Margoliouth

("The Book of the Apple," p. 191) refers to this teaching as one of several "commonplaces of medieval scholasticism," but it does not in fact correspond with any well-known doctrine of the schoolmen.
[55] See below, pp. 51-52.
[56] See below, p. 53.

[23]

is said to consist in the knowledge of God, Who made being out of nothing.[57] *The Apple* (H-L) omits, however, the dramatic appeal of the disciples for some help beyond rational argumentation to dispel their fear of dying. Instead, Symas and Melion immediately declare themselves eager to die, and the discussion of suicide—put into Melion's mouth but subsequently approved by Aristotle—follows.[58] The rejection of suicide in the Hebrew-Latin version departs from the Arabic-Persian, however, in one significant feature which may indicate neo-Platonic influence. Suicide as a means of hastening one's attainment of wisdom is recommended for the perfect, and Abraham is named as one who might justifiably have killed himself. But since the purpose of this life is the gradual achievement of philosophical perfection through self-denial, the imperfect (among whom Melion includes himself) ought to live out the fulness of their days.[59] This limited approval of suicide is reminiscent of some passages in Plotinus. For example, speaking of the Proficient's response to captivity by his enemies, Plotinus says:

> Besides in many cases captivity will certainly prove an advantage; and those that suffer have their freedom in their hands; if they stay, either there is reason in their staying, and then they have no real grievance, or they stay against reason, when they should not, and then they have themselves to blame.[60]

The passage in which Plotinus warns that premature death is not to be sought lightly is even similar verbally to Melion's like warning in *The Apple* (H-L).[61] Plotinus says:

> And if there be a period allotted to all by fate, to anticipate the hour could not be a happy act, unless, as we have indicated, under stern necessity.
> If everyone is to hold in the other world a standing determined by the state in which he quitted this, there must be no withdrawal as long as there is any hope of progress.[62]

Plotinian influence here, however, must remain conjectural. Another possibility, since the rabbi was living in Moslem Spain, lies in Margoliouth's suggestion that this opinion is taken from certain unspecified commentators on the Koran.[63]

---

[57] *Ibid.*
[58] See below, pp. 54-56.
[59] See below, p. 56.
[60] *Ennead* I, 4, 7 in Stephen MacKenna (trans.), Plotinus, *The Enneads* (London: Faber and Faber, Ltd., 1956), p. 47. Cf. also *Ennead* I, 4, 16 (MacKenna, p. 52) and *Ennead* VI, 4, 5 and 7 (MacKenna, pp. 521-524). These passages were excerpted, translated and published by Thomas Taylor, *On Suicide* (London: n.p., 1834).
[61] See below, p. 56.
[62] *Ennead* I, 9 (MacKenna, p. 79).
[63] Margoliouth, "The Book of the Apple," p. 190.

Woven into this discussion of suicide is another long interpolation which condemns ancient star-idolatry and praises Noe and Abraham as men who worshipped the true Creator and Mover of the first of the heavenly spheres.[64] The rabbi's purpose here, in having Aristotle approve of Abraham's religion and in endowing Abraham with an Aristotelian cosmology, is obviously to render the Stagyrite more acceptable to medieval Spanish Jews.

The next passage, outlining the procedure for learning philosophy and recommending sources, again somewhat parallels the Arabic version; but it is greatly condensed, with all the lively exchanges among the disciples and their forceful objections to the main argument omitted. The master recommends that one begin with his first eight books; though here unnamed, a subsequent description of their contents shows that Aristotle means his logical works.[65] These will prepare the student of philosophy to read his *De Anima*, which will bring him to the highest degree of knowledge.[66]

Aristotle repeats his plea to the disciples to restrain their desires for pleasure and reminds them that a fear of dying is a sure sign that one has not yet reached the perfection of wisdom. This passage, too, is a condensation of a similar section of *The Apple* (A-P), without the exchange of objections and solutions which that work exhibits.[67] The discussions on the need for a teacher and on the differences between good and evil men are combined in the Hebrew-Latin version into one short speech which is less reminiscent of *The Apple* (A-P) than of Aristotle's *Politics*, or, indeed, of the *Phaedo* itself, both of which distinguish between free and servile men. One class of men, those who have no wisdom of their own, are said to need teachers who will lead them in the right path like bridled beasts. This class is contrasted with the truly virtuous, who are guided by their own understanding. At this point, another interpolation appears, in which Aristotle attacks the false teachings of two sects and claims to have demolished their errors in his philosophy. They are, first, those who teach the eternity of the world, and, second, those who hold that the human soul begins and ends with the generation and death of its body. The argument of the latter that the physical weaknesses of youth, age, and illness interfere with understanding is singled out for special attention. This passage is, of course, a patent attempt to remedy the two basic errors of

---

[64] See below, pp. 54-56.
[65] See below, pp. 58-59.
[66] See below, p. 57. This description of the contents of the *De Anima* of Aristotle is not accurate; most of these questions are not treated

therein. Margoliouth says that this description fits a certain Hebrew *Book of the Soul* which I have not been able to identify.
[67] See below, pp. 52-54.

Aristotelian philosophy which medieval believers found most offensive.[68]

Finally, Aristotle refers to his *Metaphysics* as a work in which he describes the upper firmament whence the soul enters its body and to which, if unsullied by bodily pleasures, it will return after death. Unpurified souls are said to be so weighed down by material desires as to be unable to ascend—a statement which has no close parallel in the Arabic version, and yet strongly resembles the passage in the *Phaedo* where unpurified souls are said, because of their weight, to hover about the tombs of their former bodies.[69]

The most notable discrepancy between this description of how to learn philosophy and that of the Arabic version is the omission not only of Hermes and the archangels, but of any reference whatsoever to a divine revelation. Instead, the books of Aristotle—including the *Metaphysics*—have become the sole source of wisdom, which is the highest form of knowledge. The Stagyrite's position has thus been greatly elevated. The mention of the *De Anima* is an important addition in this later version; we can presume that the author of the Arabic would have included it if he had known of it. On the other hand, the Hebrew translator's omission of the titles of the logical works, and of the *Ethics*, the *Physics*, and the *Politics* need not be ascribed to ignorance. His work was hasty and careless; moreover, these titles would add nothing essential to his purpose, which was merely an exhortation to the philosophic life rather than a treatise on curriculum.

The reproduction of the death-scene, too, shows discrepancies due to haste in Chasdai's Hebrew version. Aristotle's poignant clasp of Kriton's hand is omitted, and what had been the philosopher's final prayer is mingled instead with the eulogy spoken by the disciples.[70]

Such is the final form of *The Apple*, the form which in Latin translation passed into the medieval universities all over Europe, accepted as a genuine Aristotelian work for three hundred years. The Hebrew-Latin is really a new version. It keeps the setting, the main speakers, the central theme and the dialogue structure of the Arabic-Persian book. But it is much shortened, with the psychological drama and the literary elegance of its model greatly diminished. Furthermore, the Hebrew translator has made important additions to enhance the authority of Aristotle among his contemporaries; in these interpolations, he associates the Greek philosopher very closely with Abraham, and, moreover, has him renounce what medieval Hebrew and Christian—and, indeed, Moslem—believers regarded as Aristotle's two most fla-

[68] See below, pp. 58-59.   p. 89.
[69] See below, p. 59. Cf. *Phaedo*, 81C-E,   [70] See below, p. 59.

grant errors: the eternity of the world, and the mortality of the human soul. Let us trace, now, the path through history which the various versions of this little dialogue followed.

II. The History of the The Apple (A-P)

The Apple entered the Latin Cest through a Hebrew translation from an Arabic version, but its ultimate origin has not yet been determined. Various suggestions as to authorship have been made. There are some indications that the treatise is of Greek origin. Margoliouth, for example, found the text of the Persian version written in the margin of a commentary on the *De Anima* of Aristotle[1] in a codex entitled "Translations from the Greek." He doubts, however, that there ever was a Greek version, on the grounds that the Persian reveals no mistranslations of Greek terms and moreover uses as essential parts of its arguments phrases which are borrowed from the Koran. He suggests instead a Sabaean author, as we mentioned earlier.[2] T. J. De Boer, in his history of Islamic philosophy, mentions and quotes (without giving a source) *The Apple* as an example of pseudo-Aristotelian works which were accepted by the earliest Islamic philosophers as genuine, and which thus seriously distorted Aristotle's thought. De Boer classifies *The Apple* under "late-Greek productions in which a Pythagorizing Platonism or Neo-Platonism, or even a barren syncretism was quite frankly taught." He thus says that it is a Greek work, but he gives no reasons or evidence for this opinion.[3] Louis Massignon speaks of the Arabic version, but calls it a translation *(traduction)* of an apocryphal work attributed to Aristotle, and cites Margoliouth's edition of the Persian version, which he calls a re-translation *(retraduction)*. However, he does not say what language he believes the Arabic to be based on, nor does he cite sources or give reasons for his assertion. His knowledge of the Arabic version comes from the previously mentioned *Encyclopedia* of the Brothers of Purity, and he doubts that the work can be traced to al-Kindi; no reason is given for his inclusion of the work in his section on al-Kindi.[4] S. D. Wingate, in her study of Aristotle's biological works, speaks of a Vatican manuscript dated 1288 as containing a version of *The Apple (De Pomo)* from the Greek.[5] C. H. Haskins has seen a manuscript in Seville containing a notation that

---

[1] Margoliouth cites Ousley, 95, viii, incorrectly ("The Book of the Apple," p. 188, n. 2 and p. 192). Kraemer rightly gives *ix* instead of *viii* in "Das Arabische Original," p. 486, n. 4. The manuscript is described by Ethé in his *Persian Manuscripts of the Bodleian Library* (1889), number 1422, pp. 865-66.

[2] Margoliouth, "The Book of the Apple," p. 189.

[3] T. J. De Boer, *The History of Philosophy in Islam* (London: Luzac

and Co., Ltd., 1961. Reprint of 1903 edition), pp. 24-25.

[4] Louis Massignon, *Recueil de texts inédits concernant l'histoire de la mystique en pays d'Islam* (Paris: Librairie Orientaliste Paul Geuthner, 1929), p. 178 and p. 186. The Arabic title for *The Apple* here reads *Risalat al-toffahah*.

[5] S. D. Wingate, *The Medieval Latin Versions of the Aristotelian Scientific Corpus, with Special Reference to the Biological Works* (London:

the version of the *De Pomo* therein was made from Greek into Latin.[6] Chasdai, in his prologue to the Hebrew translation from Arabic, simply states without giving evidence that the work was composed by Greek sages.[7] Hermann Gollancz, in the introduction to his English translation ot the Hebrew, is unwilling to accept this statement at its face value, but makes no attempt to solve the problem of Greek authorship.[8] Isidor Kalisch, on the other hand, the other recent translator of the treatise from Hebrew into English, accepts the work as a genuine Aristotelian treatise. He says, "This work is generally admitted to be genuine. He composed it when he was teaching at the *Lykeion* (Lyceum) in Athens."[9] Manfred of Sicily, who translated the Hebrew of Chasdai into Latin, says in his preface that the work was not composed by Aristotle himself but by the disciples who conversed with him on his death-bed.[10]

There was, in fact, a rather extended controversy among the Latin schoolmen over the Aristotelian authorship of *The Apple*. The question was involved in the larger debate about whether Aristotle was saved. Those who would consign Aristotle to hell are glad to reject *The Apple* as spurious. Chief among these is an anonymous Franciscan whose disputed question, "*Utrum Aristoteles sit Salvatus?*" ("Wehther Aristotle Was Saved?") reaches a flatly negative conclusion. His opinion of *The Apple* is expressed thus: "That book [i.e. *Secretum Secretorum*] and the other called Aristotle's *The Apple* are not authentic."[11] Peter of Phylagyres, who reigned briefly as Pope Alexander V (1409-10), agreed with this opinion. He says, in his commentary on the *Sentences*, ". . . thus it is strongly believed by many that he [Aristotle] never wrote said book *(De pomo sive de morte Aristotelis)*. And the same holds true as regards the book called *De secreto secretorum.* . . ."[12]

The Courier Press, 1931), p. 23. The manuscript is *AL* 1717. Professor Wingate states that all the items in this codex containing the standard corpus of the natural works are from the Greek, with the exception of the pseudo-Aristotelian *De Plantis* and *De differentia Spiritus et Animae*. Cf. p. 22. She thus includes *The Apple* as from Greek.

6 Charles Homer Haskins, *Studies in the History of Medieval Science*, second edition (Cambridge: Harvard University Press, 1927), p. 269, n. 13. The codex, *AL* 1185, dated 1268, contains several works by al-Kindi, al-Farabi, and Ptolemy, as well as Proclus' *Elementatio Theologica*.

7 Cf. Gollancz, *The Targum to the 'Song of Songs,'* etc., p. 91 (quoted above, p. 22, n. 48.

8 *Ibid.*, p. 5.

9 Kalisch, *Ha-Tapuach: The Apple* p. iv. Kalisch's title calls the work a *Treatise on the Immortality of the Soul by Aristotle the Stagyrite*.

10 See below, p. 50.

11 Anton-Hermann Chroust, "A Contribution to the Medieval Discussion: Utrum Aristoteles Sit Salvatus," *Journal of the History of Ideas*, 6 (1945), p. 234, n. 9. The manuscript is *Vatican Lat.* 1012, fol. 27. Both of the works mentioned here ascribe ideas to Aristotle which would favor his salvation.

12 I am quoting Chroust's translation

The opposite opinion—that *The Apple* is a genuine work and proof that Aristotle died in a spirit of Christian repentance and faith—was amazingly widespread and enduring. One of the prominent fifteenth-century Thomists at Cologne, Albert de Monte (or Lambert of Cologne), wrote a highly favorable treatise *De Salute Aristotelis (On Aristotle's Salvation)* in which, purportedly quoting from *The Apple,* he gives the exclamation *"O Ens Entium, miserere mei"* ("Oh Entity of Entities, have mercy on me") as Aristotle's last words.[13] The use of this name for the Divinity would make his supposed conversion to Christianity complete and unmistakable.

Another work, a long poem which glorifies Aristotle to the point of calling him inerrant and an indispensable forerunner of Christ, quotes this same version of Aristotle's last words. The poem, entitled *Liber de vita et morte Aristotelis metrice conscriptus cum glossa inter-linarea (The Book of Aristotle's Life and Death, Written in Verse with an Inter-Lineal Gloss)* contains a versification of *The Apple* as its last segment; it comes from the same school at Cologne, and is—in Chroust's opinion—probably by Lambert himself.[14]

Two Polish scholars of the fourteenth and fifteenth centuries are known to have accepted *The Apple* as genuinely Aristotelian. The first rector of the restored University of Cracow, in a eulogy for bishop-elect Peter Wysz in the year 1392, uses the phrase, "As Aristotle says in the little book on the apple and his death." In the next century, Nicolaus of Blonie, an alumnus of Cracow, said in a sermon, "Aristotle says that the intellective soul is distinguished from the vegetative as

(p. 234, n. 9) of Fr. Ehrle, *Der Sentenzenkommentar Peters von Candia,* Beiheft ix (1925) of *Franziskanische Studien,* p. 67.

[13] Chroust, "A Contribution, . . ." pp. 235-36. Chroust cites here an incunabulum from the Munich Staatsbibliothek (no date or publisher given) which I have not seen. The phrase is also said to appear in some (unspecified) manuscripts of *The Apple.*

[14] *Ibid.,* pp. 237-38 and notes 20 and 21. Plezia (*Liber de Pomo,* pp. 13-14) concurs in this opinion. The text of this poem is not easy to come by. No manuscripts are extant; Plezia cites ten early printings: GKW 2469-2477 and GKW 2498. Most scholars cite the fragment of it from C. A. Heumann's *Acta Phi-*

losophorum (Halle, 1724), which I have not seen. Thus Chroust ("A Contribution, . . ." pp. 237-38), Ingemar Düring (*Aristotle in the Ancient Biographical Tradition.* Goteborg: Elanders Boktryckeri Aktiebolag, 1957, pp. 167-68), Kraemer ("Das Arabische Original," p. 485, n. 4), and Plezia (*Liber de Pomo,* pp. 13-14). Kraemer quotes one couplet which seems to give the flavor of the poem:
> *Huius adhuc modicum pomi*
> *relevabor odore*
> *Atque docebo vos magno*
> *absque labore.*
(I shall be somewhat sustained by the fragrance of this apple, and I shall teach you without any great distress.)

the incorruptible from the corruptible. And the same thing is well put in the book *On the Apple and His Death.*[15]

In Italy, the same tendency to canonize Aristotle was found. A literary critic of the fifteenth century, Ludovico Caelio Rhodigino (Ricchieri), born in 1450, says in his *Lectiones Antiquae (Ancient Readings)* that Aristotle achieved the true Christian spirit at his death, weeping in sorrow yet trusting in the mercy of the Sublime Entity.[16] Aristotle's supposed final prayer also appears in J. J. Beurer's life of Aristotle, published at Basle in 1587;[17] this eulogy contains, according to Ingemar Düring, several incredibly stupid remarks which show the low state of transalpine Greek studies in the late sixteenth century.[18] The ejaculation can also be seen in an eighteenth century inscription at Westminster Abbey, on the tomb of the Duke of Buckingham in the Henry VII chapel,[19] and as a substitute for the usual Latin epitaph concluding Karl Julius Weber's *Demokritus XII* (Stuttgart, 1841), p. 265.[20]

Those who knew only the Arabic version also disagreed about the authenticity of the work. The Brothers of Purity, whose tenth century encyclopedia contains the earliest known certain reference to *The Apple,* consider it a genuine work of Aristotle.[21] Its theme, that the soul originates in the heavens and strives through wisdom to return

---

[15] Cf. Plezia, *Liber de Pomo*, p. 14. The dialogue does not in fact make this distinction. Plezia cites here an edition of the sermons of Nicolaus which appeared in Cologne in 1613, *tomus* I, p. 71.

[16] Hertz, "Das Buch vom Apfel," p. 397. Apparently there is no modern edition of these *Readings;* a recent history of Italian literary criticism cites a 1516 edition (Weinberg, Bernard. *A History of Literary Criticism in the Italian Renaissance.* Chicago: University of Chicago Press, 1961, p. 1122). Hertz found the ejaculation, "O Ens Entium, miserere mei," cited in two other sources which I could not investigate: Matthäus Hammer, *Rosetum historiarum* (Zwickau, 1657), and Joh. Henr. Ursinus, *Acerra philologica*, Lib. I, c. 50 (no date or place of publication).

[17] Hertz, "Das Buch vom Apfel," p. 396.

[18] *Aristotle in the Ancient Biographical Tradition*, p. 179.

[19] Hertz, "Das Buch vom Apfel," p.

397, n. 7.

[20] *Ibid.* This supposed phrase from *The Apple* ("Oh Entity of Entities") was gradually combined with another Christianizing version of Aristotle's last words; this earlier and indedendent tradition began with a Dominican Father-General, Humbert of Romans, in the mid-thirteenth century. Hertz traces the history of this tradition prior to its synthesis with that from *The Apple* on pp. 395-97 of "Das Buch vom Apfel."

[21] It is difficult to assemble much certain information about either the brothers of Purity (Ikhwan As-Safa) or their so-called *Encyclopedia (Rasa'il).* They were a secret society, and their writings were burned during a persecution. A recent survey of research on this question points out that there is no agreement yet on the exact date and place of publication of their writings, nor on their authorship. Approximate conclusions put them in Basra in the tenth century. Cf. A. L. Tibawi, "Ikhwan As-Safa and their *Rasa'il*, A Critical

there, is one of their chief tenets.[22] *The Apple* is also mentioned favorably in the early thirteenth-century correspondence of Frederick II of Sicily with Ibn Sabin. Frederick, as was his custom, sent some questions which his own scholars could not answer to ar-Rashid, the Caliph of Morocco, who forwarded them to Ibn Sabin in Ceuta. Among them were questions on the eternity of matter and the immortality of the soul; Frederick asked specifically about Aristotle's reasons for holding the eternity of the world. In his reply, Ibn Sabin quoted from *The Apple* to show that Aristotle had changed his opinion on those two key questions.[23] *The Apple* is also quoted by the anyonymous author (perhaps Samuel bar Jakob) of an Arabic treatise on battle rules, and is praised by Abraham ibn Ezra,[24] cited by both as an authentic work.

On the other side, the later copyists of the Arabic version of *The Apple*, apparently finding it impossible to attribute to Aristotle the ideas therein, substitute Socrates as the main interlocutor, thus denying

Review of a Century and a Half of Research," in pp. 28-45 of *The Islamic Quarterly*, vol. 2 (1955).

The *Encyclopedia* as a whole has not been translated into a western language, but the passage which mentions *The Apple* is given by F. H. Dieterici in his *Die Philosophie der Araber im X. Jahrhundert n. Chr.* (Leipzig: J. C. Hinrichs'sche Buchhandlung, 1876), *Erster Theil*, p. 105. It reads: "Aristotle, the Master of Logic, holds the same view in his letter which is known under the name of *The Apple*, in his words at his death, discussing the primacy of philosophy. For the philosopher will be rewarded for his philosophy after the separation of the soul from the body." (My translation of Dieterici's German).

There is also evidence that *The Apple* was known to Islamic thinkers in tenth-century Iran. The long lost philosophical writings of al-Razi, who was famous throughout the middle ages as a physician, are recently coming to light; these show that one of his opponents in a debate, Nasir-e-Khosraw, mentions Aristotle in *The Book of the Apple* as commending his soul to "the lord of the souls of philosophers" at his death. Al-Razi was born at Ray

(near Teheran) around 864 and died there around 930. Cf. Corbin, *Histoire de la philosophie Islamique*, vol. I, pp. 194-99. Corbin gives no details about the source of this reference to *The Apple*. Educated Persians could have used either an Arabic or a Persian version.

[22] De Lacy O'Leary, *How Greek Science Passed to the Arabs* (London: Routledge and Kegan Paul, Ltd., 1949), pp. 179-180.

[23] Haskins, *Studies in Medieval Science*, p. 264, n. 119. This correspondence, which became famous as "The Sicilian Questions," is quoted (in Arabic) and summarized (in French) by A. F. Mehren, "Correspondence du philosophe soufi ibn Sabin Abd Oul-Haqq avec l'Empéreur Frédéric II de Hohenstaufen," *Journal Asiatique*, vii série, tome xiv (Oct.-Dec. 1879), pp. 341-454. Sabin lists *The Apple* among Aristotle's metaphysical works, and says repeatedly that Aristotle held the immortality of the soul. Kraemer ("Das Arabische Original," p. 487, n. 6), also quotes this passage (in Arabic).

[24] Steinschneider, *Hebraeische Übersetzungen*, p. 267. I could not trace the sources cited here.

Aristotelian authorship.[25] Earlier, Moses Maimonides, chief of those twelfth-century Jewish authors who knew the work, states that it is spurious. In a letter to his translator, Samuel ibn Tibbon, where he sets forth which philosophical works are worth studying and which ought to be ignored, he says,

> Among the works which you mention as being in your possession, you name *De Pomo* [sic] and *The Golden House*. These two treatises are spurious, and entirely valueless: they are among those which are ascribed to Aristotle, but which are not genuine.[26]

There is, however, a strong and enduring Jewish tradition of glorifying Aristotle, paralleling that of the Latin authors, in which our dialogue also plays a part. The story goes that Alexander the Great, having acquired the writings of King Solomon in his conquest of Jerusalem, sent them to Aristotle, who as a result renounced philosophy and became a proselyte. In a supposed letter to Alexander announcing his conversion, Aristotle refers to a book in which he recants his previous stance of denying a life after death and affirming the eternity of the world. This letter is still extant in Hebrew. The book by Aristotle to which it refers (*The Apple*, of course) is mentioned by Hayyim of Briviesca, who says that Abraham Ibn Ezra had received it from Ibn al-Khatib, who died in 1370.[27]

This recognition of *The Apple* as a genuine work also won acceptance for Aristotle among the cabalists. Moses Botarel, for example, who saw only a verbal distinction between philosophy and the cabal, welcomed the work and, on its basis, assigned Aristotle a place in Paradise.[28]

The denial of Aristotle's authorship is, of course, the opinion that finally prevailed. Despite the wide acceptance of the treatise in the medieval universities—of which we shall see more later—it had almost no influence on the great scholastics. Since the middle ages, and up to Plezia's edition of the text in 1954, there are only four known printings of the Latin version, all of them incunabula. And of these, only two are in editions of Aristotle's works.[29] Wenrich, in his pioneer work of cataloguing the Oriental versions of Greek works, lists it as a Greek

---

[25] Cf. Kraemer, "Das Arabische Original," pp. 488-489.

[26] From H. Adler (ed.), *Miscellany of Hebrew Literature* (London: N. Trubner and Co., 1872), vol. I, p. 225. Cf. Steinschneider, *H.Ü.*, p. 41 and pp. 415-418.

[27] Louis Ginzberg, "Aristotle in Jewish Legend," *The Jewish Encyclopedia*, vol. II (New York: Ktav Publishing House, Inc., 1901), p. 99.

[28] Steinschneider, *H.Ü.*, p. 269, n. 1157, citing a manuscript of Botarel's commentary on *Jezirah*. Cf. also Ginzberg, *loc. cit.*, and Hertz, "Das Buch vom Apfel," p. 372.

[29] *GKW* 2336 and 2341. See above, p. 8, n. 21.

work falsely attributed to Aristotle.[30] And Dieterici, in a note on the reference to the work by The Brothers of Purity, says that it is spurious.[31]

Speculation about non-Greek authorship is, then, to be expected. Along these lines, there are suggestions of Moslem, Jewish, and Christian authors. One notable opinion, held by Brockelmann and, after him, Jörg Kraemer, is that al-Kindi wrote the treatise.[32] This suggestion is plausible doctrinally, for al-Kindi did hold, in opposition to his Greek predecessors and later Arabic philosophers, the creation of the world in time by God. He defined creation as the act of making being out of nothing, a formula which coincides perfectly with that found in *The Apple*.[33] Al-Kindi, moreover, taught the immortality of the soul and preserved a fragment of Aristotle's *Eudemus*, an early Platonizing dialogue in which the Stagyrite holds the doctrine of immortality.[34] While the title, *The Book of the Apple*, does not appear on any of the ancient lists of nearly 300 works attributed to al-Kindi, one of his titles is *A Treatise on the Soul, its Unity, its Simplicity, its Independence of the Body*.[35] While this would be a plausible title for our work, these topics are commonplaces in peripatetic psychology, and we can conclude nothing without examining the work itself. Armand Abel says that *The Apple* is mentioned in the works of al-Kindi, and that it was retranslated at Baghdad in the tenth century. However, he gives no

---

[30] Johannes Georgius Wenrich, *De Auctorum Graecorum Versionibus et Commentariis Syriacis Arabicis Armenicis Persicisque* (Lipsiae: 1842), p. 138.

[31] *Die Philosophie der Araber*, p. 226.

[32] Kraemer, "Das Arabische Original," p. 505. The earlier instance which I could find of the attribution of *The Apple* to al-Kindi is the one referred to above (p. 28) by Louis Massignon, who gives no reason for the suggestion and also states that al-Kindi's authorship is doubtful. Brockelmann simply includes the work, without comment, in his entry on al-Kindi, and cites the same places in Massignon and Margoliouth which I have used. Cf. C. Brockelmann, *Geschichte der Arabischen Litteratur*. Erster Supplementband (Leiden: E. J. Brill, 1937), p. 373.

[33] In *The Apple*, for example, God the Creator is described as "He Who made being out of nothing and Who is the Beginner of all Beginnings and the Origin of all Origins." (Cf. below, p. 54). Al-Kindi's words, from his *First Philosophy*, are: "The One, the Real, is then the First, the Creator from nothing Who maintains in existence What He has created from nothing." Cited in Richard Walzer, *Greek to Arabic. Essays on Islamic Philosophy* (Cambridge: Harvard University Press, 1962), p. 188. Most of the monographs in this book are reprinted from various journals.

[34] Walzer, *ibid.*, p. 201. Cf., for example, "Theories of the Soul in the Early Aristotle," by D. A. Rees, in *Aristotle and Plato in the Mid-Fourth Century*, eds. I. Düring and G. E. L. Owen (Goteborg: n.p., 1960), pp. 191-200.

[35] G. Flugel, *Al-Kindi gennant der Philosoph der Araber* (Leipzig: F. A. Brockhaus, 1857), p. 30.

references, nor does he say from what language or into what language the retranslation was done.[36] Al-Kindi's authorship, then, remains conjectural.

A Jewish author is suggested by Dieterici,[37] by Losius,[38] and by Steinschneider;[39] this opinion is based on the passage about Noah and Abraham as the revealers of the true Creator. While subsequent scholarship has shown this passage to be an interpolation made by Chasdai, in translating the work from Arabic to Hebrew, there is nothing in the older Arabic version to preclude a Hebrew origin for the work. The reference to Hermes near the end could easily be an interpolation; if it is omitted, the doctrine of the dialogue is not affected.

Finally, there is a flat statement by Erasmus that the work was written by a Christian. In one of his letters to John More, which later became a preface to an edition of the complete works of Aristotle which was published in Basle in 1531, he says, "The book *De Pomo* is plainly by a Christian man."[40] But he gives no grounds for this opinion. Erasmus refers, of course, to the Latin version.

The Arabic version is, then, as far as is certainly known, the original form of *The Apple*. References to it by the Brothers of Purity, by Cbn Sabin, and by Maimonides, Steinschneider's discovery of a fragment of it, and Margoliouth's discovery of the Persian translation all encouraged the search for the Arabic text itself. This text was found to be extant in three copies, though all of them late—fourteenth to sixteenth centuries. This text is the subject of Kraemer's 1956 monograph, "Das Arasbische original. . . ."

The first of the three copies is an abbreviated version, entitled *Muhtasar Kitab at-Tuffaha (Abridgment of the Book of the Apple),* in a Christian-Arabic codex at Cairo which dates from the fourteenth or fifteenth century.[41] The dialogue, which is on folios 248-267, has Socrates rather than Aristotle as the main speaker; it is of little value in establishing the text of the lost original. A second, more complete version, also with Socrates as the hero, was discovered early in this century by a Syrian scholar, Amin Zahir Hairallah, in the library of

[36] Armand Abel, *Aristote, La légende et l'histoire* (Bruxelles: Office de Publicité, 1944), p. 71.

[37] *Die Philos. der Araber,* I. 1876, p. 226.

[38] According to the report of D. S. Margoliouth, in "The Book of the Apple," p. 189.

[39] Steinschneider, *Hebraeischen Übersetzungen,* p. xvii.

[40] P. S. Allen (ed.), *Opvs Epistolarvm Des. Erasmi Roterdami* (Oxonii: in Typographeo Clarendoniano, MCM-XXXVIII), Vol. IX, p. 138.

[41] The codex is *Taimuriyya ahlaq* 290. Its history and contents are said to be given in Paul Kraus' introduction to an edition from the same manuscript of an abridgment of Galen's *Peri Ethon,* which appeared in the *Bulletin of the Faculty of Arts* of the University of Egypt, V, i (1937), pp. 1-51. Cited by Kraemer, "Das Arabische Original," p. 488, n. 2.

the Greek patriarchate of Antioch at Damascus. Kraemer says that the manuscript of this version contains so many and such extensive paraphrases and additions that it, too, is an unreliable basis on which to establish the original text. The printing of this version, whose title is *Kitab Suqrat al-hakim al-ma'ruf bi-t-Tuffaha qalahu 'inda wafatihi (The Book of Socrates the Sage, known as The Book of the Apple, Which He Dictated at the Time of His Death)*, in the journal *al-Muqtataf (The Gleanings)*, contains further additions and alterations; no information about the age or condition of the manuscript is given.[42]

The third, the most important and reliable of the three manuscripts, was recognized for the first time by Kraemer in a sixteenth century codex at Istanbul, where the title is *ar-Risala al-ma'rufa bi-t-Tuffaha Li-Aristatalis (The Epistle known as The Apple, by Aristotle)*.[43] The codex is a miscellany of 194 folios, containing (pseudo-) Greek, (pseudo-) Persian and Arabic proverbs, anecdotes, admonitions, etc.

The text of *The Apple* is on folios 170b-181b, interspersed between passages of Hunain's *Adab-al-falasifa (The Conduct of the Philosophers)*, and—as may be seen by the title—is here rightly attributed to Aristotle.[44] Kraemer states that this version, though the latest of all— even later than the Persian, Hebrew, and Latin translations—and thus full of doctrinal and scribal errors, is nevertheless the most reliable and closest to the Arabic original. He bases this conclusion on two facts. First, a passage in this Istanbul manuscript coincides perfectly with the previously known fragment in the codex at the Bodleian Library which Margoliouth had used to authenticate the Persian translation.[45] The other two Arabic manuscripts, i.e. those at Cairo and Damascus, coincide substantially with the Istanbul version in this passage.[46] Secondly, the rest of the Istanbul version and the rest of Margoliouth's Persian text correspond so closely to each other that they can be used for mutual correction. While the Cairo and Damascus manuscripts of the Arabic differ from these in several particulars, they are substantially copies of the same work.[47] The fact that the Persian version contains many transliterations of Arabic terms and

---

[42] The text is in vol. 55 (1919), pp. 475-484 and vol. 56 (1920), pp. 18-22 and 105-110 and 217-221 of *al-Muqtataf (Gleanings)*. Cf. Kraemer, "Das Arabische Original," p. 488 and n. 2.

[43] Kraemer, *loc. cit.*, pp. 489-490. The codex is *Köprülü* 1608.

[44] It is immediately preceded by a copy of Alexander's *Second Letter of Consolation* to his mother. *Ibid.*, p. 490.

[45] Cf. above, p. 18, n. 39. Kraemer reminds us here that the fragment had

been recognized by Steinschneider in his *Catal. Librorum Hebr. in Bibl. Bodleiana* (Berlin, 1852-60), p. 675. Cf. "Das Arabische Original," p. 491 and n. 1. Kraemer here also gives the title of the treatise in which the fragment is found: the anonymous *Risalat al-Burhan fi tadkiyat al-hayawan (Epistle of Demonstration Concerning the Rousing of Animals)*.

[46] *Ibid.*, pp. 491-492.

[47] *Ibid.*

phrases leads Kraemer to believe that the Persian is derived from an early Arabic archetype, rather than the extant Arabic text being a translation of the Persian, and this despite the fact that all the extant Arabic manuscripts are of later date than the Persian.[48]

Such, then, is the story of our dialogue prior to its entrance into medieval Europe by way of a Hebrew and then a Latin translation. There are interesting but inconclusive indications that the original version was Greek; in fact, the treatise found acceptance as a genuine Aristotelian work among Islamic, Jewish, and Latin authors. Those who rightly reject Aristotle as author have suggested al-Kindi instead, as well as certain unspecified Jewish, Christian, and Sabaean writers. Internal evidence does not, at first glance, solve the question, because the doctrine is compatible with the deeply different world-views of all of these. And historical evidence to date is inconclusive. Thus, as far as we know, the Arabic version, subsequently translated into Hebrew and Persian and thence into Latin, Italian, German, Swedish, and English, is the original composition. But though the dialogue was known as early as the tenth century, extant Arabic manuscripts date only from the fourteenth and sixteenth centuries. The fact that the treatise was still being copied four to six hundred years after its first composition testifies to its great popularity in the medieval world of Islam. All in all, we can be sure that much of its history during these centuries awaits our future discovery. And definite proof of earlier Greek and even Syriac versions would not be surprising, for such is the general pattern of transmission of philosophical works from Greece to the West.

[48] *Ibid.*, pp. 492-493. I do not understand Kraemer's thirteenth century date for the Persian text, which he does not explain. He cites Ethé's catalogue (*Persian Manuscripts of the Bodleian Library*, 1889, p. 865), where a date of 1630 is clearly and definitely given for the Persian translation of the *De Anima* of Aristotle therein. Since the Persian translation of *The Apple* is written in the margin of this work, it could hardly have been made some 400 years earlier. At any rate, Ethé's date confirms Kraemer's conclusion that the Persian version of *The Apple* derives from the Arabic, and not the Arabic from the Persian.

Kraemer here cites S. W. Bacher, *Nizami's Leben und Werke*, (Leipzig, 1871, p. 120) for the suggestion that Nizami—a thirteenth century poet—knew the Persian version of *The Apple;* this is still possible, inasmuch as another manuscript of the (a?) Persian text does date back to the thirteenth century. Cf. above, p. 6, n. 17.

Nizami's poem deals with the search for the fountain of life by Alexander the Great, and the description of Aristotle's death, in the second part of the poem, is said to be based on *The Apple* The first part of the poem has been translated into English: *The Sikander Nama, E. Bara, or Book of Alexander the Great. Written A.D. 1200 by Abu Muhammed bin Yusef bin Mu Ayyid-C-Nisami' d-Din.* Trans. H. Wilberforce Clarke (London: W. H. Allen and Co.), 1881.

III. The Manuscript Tradition of the Latin Version of the Apple.

The Latin version of *The Apple* enjoyed an honored place in the standard course of instruction in the medieval universities for some three hundred years. This version, translated from Chasdais Hebrew, came from the court of Manfred in Sicily in the mid-thirteenth century. Its fantastic popularity is obvious from the fact that ninety manuscripts of it were known as of 1961, when the most recent volume of *Aristoteles Latinus* was published. And one hesitates to call this figure final because of the rate at which manuscripts of the *De Pomo* have come to light in recent times. Thus *Aristoteles Latinus, pars prior,* listed thirty-seven in 1939. In 1955, the second volume, *pars posterior,* listed thirty-three more (including one doubtful fragment). Plezia's conspectus at the end of his 1960 edition of the text adds seventeen others, two of which were recently lost. And the 1961 *Supplementum Altera* of *Aristoteles Latinus,* the most recent volume, lists sixteen of these (including one of the lost ones) and adds five others.[1] In addition to these, Jörg Kraemer mentions a Berlin manuscript (*AL* 802) as containing the *De Pomo,* a fact not noted in the incomplete description of that codex in *Aristoteles Latinus.*[2] Thus a total of ninety-three manuscripts of the *De Pomo* have been known in recent times; subtracting the two since lost and the one dubious fragment, we have extant, according to present knowledge, ninety manuscripts of our work. Its geographical spread is broad; these manuscripts are to be found in Austria, Belgium, Czechoslovakia, England, France, Germany, Italy, Poland, Spain, Switzerland, the United States and the Vatican.

There has been some controversy about the identity of the translator. The prologue names Manfred himself,[3] but Steinschneider doubted that the young king or any other Christian of his time would have had a sufficient knowledge of Hebrew.[4] Chroust[5] and Abel[6] attribute the translation to Bartholomew of Messana, but do not give

---

[1] The dubious fragment is in *AL* 1513. The two which Plezia marks as recently lost are *AL* 110 and #37 on his own conspectus (never catalogued in *AL*), *Parthenopolitanus, Bibliothecae urbicae* 134 Oct. 15e. Plezia's conspectus contains two printing errors: his #45, *AL* 1111, should read *AL* 1011, and his #81, *AL* 1788, should read *AL* 1798.

[2] Kraemer, "Das Arabische Original," pp. 484-85 and p. 495. On p. 495 he mentions a Paris manuscript *Bibliotheque National* 4° *Rés. R*

1512 as the source of the *editio princeps.* This mode of reference is so different from that in *Aristoteles Latinus* that it is impossible to determine whether this coincides with one of the items therein. It may, then, be a ninety-first manuscript.

[3] Cf. *The Apple or Aristotle's Death,* below, p. 49.

[4] *Hebraeische Übersetzungen,* p. 268.

[5] "A Contribution," p. 235.

[6] *Aristote, La légende et l'histoire,* p. 71. Plezia is puzzled by this suggestion, as Bartholomew translated

[38]

reasons. Lynn Thorndike[7] mentions the problem but takes no position, while Maurice De Wulf asserts Manfred to be the translator.[8] Plezia favors taking the prologue at face-value, first, because the translator was no great Hebrew expert; he misreads and distorts the sense of the text in three places.[9] Moreover, Jewish amanuenses were available at Manfred's court and were frequently used for such tasks.[10] Furthermore, the titles by which the translator refers to himself in the prologue are in the same formula that Manfred is known to have used on other occasions: "Son of the divine and august emperor Frederick, by the grace of God prince of Taranto, lord of the mountain of honor, Sant Angelo, and governor-general of the illustrious Conrad, the second king of Sicily."[11] Manfred, having received these titles in his father's will in December, 1250, is known to have used them in 1255, 1256, and 1257. On August 10, 1258, he became king and was thereafter called *rex*. These facts would place the translation sometime between 1250 and 1258. Two authors suggest that it was done at Santo Gervasio in the summer or fall of 1255.[12] That Manfred did thus translate the *De Pomo* is consistent with what is known from other sources about his philosophical interests.[13] And finally, as Plezia points out, the distinctive style of the prologue is very like that of some of Manfred's certainly genuine letters.[14] All in all, there seems no sufficient reason to doubt his authorship of the Latin version.

from Greek rather than Arabic. Perhaps Abel, who calls the Arabic version a translation, knows of a Greek version. See above, pp. 33-34 and Plezia, *Liber De Pomo*, p. 21.

[7] In his *A History of Magic and Experimental Science*, vol. II (New York: The MacMillan Company, 1923), p. 930; cf. also pp. 254-55.

[8] In his *Histoire de la philosophie médiévale*, tome II (Louvain: Institut Supérieur de Philosophie, 1936), p. 44.

[9] See *The Apple, or Aristotle's Death*, below, pp. 55-56 and corresponding notes.

[10] Plezia, *Liber De Pomo*, pp. 21-22. Cf. also Haskins, *Studies in the History of Medieval Science*, p. 278 and p. 283. Lucien Leclerc, who accepts Manfred's authorship, observes that Manfred would have had a better knowledge of Arabic and thus suggests that the Hebrew version was the only one available to

him. Cf. his *Histoire de la médicine arabe*, II (Paris, 1876), p. 462.

[11] Cf. *The Apple, or Aristotle's Death*, below, p. 49.

[12] Plezia, *Liber De Pomo*, p. 21 and pp. 65-66. I could not obtain the sources which Plezia cites for this information: Böhmer-Fischer, *Regesta imperii* V. 1 (Innsbruck, 1879), nr. 4653 and F. Schirrmacher, *Die letzten Hohenstaufen* (Göttingen, 1871), pp. 212-216.

[13] He sponsored Peter of Hibernia's dispute, "Whether the members were made for the sake of their operations, or operations were made for the sake of the members?" Cf. Plezia, *Liber De Pomo*, p. 22. Cf. also Haskins, *Studies in the History of Medieval Science*, pp. 269-270, where we are reminded that Manfred was praised for his knowledge both of philosophy and languages by an Egyptian visitor to his court.

[14] Plezia, *Liber De Pomo*, p. 22.

A study of the provenance and present location of manuscripts shows a preponderantly French influence. French libraries now have twenty of the known ninety manuscripts, more than any other country. Of those whose origin has been determined, Plezia lists ten which were done by French scribes and are now located outside of that country.[15] *Aristoteles Latinus* lists eleven manuscripts now outside of France as being of French origin; eight of these are on Plezia's list, two are not, while one (*AL* 1798) is described as French by Plezia and as English by the editors of *Aristoteles Latinus*. Thus, out of the ninety known manuscripts, thirty-one or thirty-two were written in France and/or are now located there. This strong French background is plausible in view of the fact that in December of 1263 Manfred sent to the University of Paris a large collection of philosophical works which had been translated from Greek and Arabic at his court.[16] The letter accompanying this collection[17] mentions no titles, but it is fair to assume that *The Apple*, which could be loosely described as a translation from Arabic (or, perhaps, Greek), would have been included. Manfred speaks in the prologue of his desire to have the book more widely known among Christians.[18] The general attitude toward Aristotle by this date, both within and without the universities, was so amicable that a work in which he purportedly repudiates his two most serious errors and dies in the attitude of a Christian believer would have found ready acceptance. As evidence of the positive official attitude in the universities, we have an outline composed between 1230 and 1240 by an anonymous Parisian master to aid students in preparing for their examinations. It lists the following Aristotelian and Pseudo-Aristotelian works: *Metaphysica vetus, Metaphysica nova, Liber de Causis, Physica, De Caelo, De Generatione, Meteora, De Plantis, De Animalibus, De Anima, Parva Naturalia, Ethica Nova, Ethica Vetus, Kategorica, Perihermeneias, Analytica Priora, Analytica Posteriora, Topica, Elenchia.*[19] Moreover, a statute of the Faculty of Arts at the University of Paris, dated 1255, prescribes as required texts all the items on the above list as well as the *De Differentia Spiritus et Animae;* this statute was probably just an official recognition of what was by then a well established practice.[20] Granted such an intellectual climate and Manfred's

---

[15] In his conspectus at the end of *Liber De Pomo*, pp. 72-78.

[16] Denifié-Chatelain, *Chartularium Universitatis Parisiensis*, I (Paris, 1889), no. 394, pp. 435-436.

[17] *Ibid.* This letter betrays striking stylistic similarities to the translator's prologue to *The Apple*, as Plezia points out (*Liber de Pomo*, pp. 23-

24).

[18] See *The Apple, or Aristotle's Death*, below, p. 49.

[19] Martin Grabmann, *I divieti ecclesiastici di Aristotele sotto Innocenzo III e Gregorio IX* (Romae: Typis Pontificiae Universitatis Gregorianae, 1941), pp. 113-127.

[20] Pierre Mandonnet, O.P., *Siger de*

admiration for *The Apple,* it seems very likely that the dialogue would have been included in his donation to the university in 1263.

At any rate, once in France the treatise was rapidly and carelessly copied and widely circulated. Of our ninety manuscripts, sixteen are dated in the thirteenth century; two of these are said to be of French origin, two of Italian, and two of English; of those whose provenance is not known, five are now in France, two in Italy, and one each in London, Cracow, and Switzerland. Seven others are dated thirteenth to fourteenth century; one of these is of French birth, one of Italian, and one of English; the remaining four are now found in Paris, Seville, Mainz, and New York. The greatest number of our manuscripts, fifty-two, were written in the fourteenth century; eight of these were produced in France, three in Germany, and one in either Italy or Spain. Their present locations are France (in fourteen cases), Germany (ten of them), Italy (nine manuscripts), England and the Vatican (five each), Czechoslovakia (for three of them), and Austria, Spain, and Poland (two each). The next century, the fifteenth, saw the production of thirteen of our ninety manuscripts; of these, five are now in Italian libraries, four in England, three in Poland, and one in Berlin. The dissemination of *The Apple,* then, was rapid throughout all of western Europe.[21]

That *The Apple* enjoyed an honored place in the medieval universities is even more evident from a collation of the information in *Aristoteles Latinus* concerning the contents of the codices in which our treatise is found. Time and again we find it bound in with Aristotle's natural works—much more frequently than with other Arabic works; nor is it merely tacked on at the end as a sort of entertainment. It is right in the midst of the most seriously studied treatises, so that we must conclude that—despite its absence from the official lists—it was included in the then standard corpus of Aristotelian works.

Birkenmajer's survey of some sixty-three works which were attributed to Aristotle in the middle ages provides a convenient frame-

Brabant et l'Averroisme Latin au XIIIme siècle, vol. I (Louvain: Institut supérieur de philosophie de l'université, 1911), p. 24.

21 The haste with which the treatise was copied is shown also by the extensive corruption of the text in the early manuscripts. Fifteen of the manuscripts which date before 1353 are so negligent that Plezia can say the scribes rewrote the treatise rather than copying it — ". . . potius rescribant quam describant." One

Vatican manuscript dated 1284—scarcely thirty years after Manfred's translation—is full of errors and lacunae. Cf. Plezia, *Liber de Pomo,* p. 24 and pp. 31-32. The main manuscript for Plezia's edition is now in Poland, but is of Italian provenance; Plezia quite plausibly suggests that the Italian tradition, though later than the French, is closer to the original. Cf. his "Neues zum pseudo-aristotelischen *Buch Vom Apfel,*" pp. 195-196.

work for this information.[22] Having arranged these works into twelve classes, according to descending degrees of authenticity, he put *De Pomo (The Apple)* into class IX—spurious works of Oriental origin—along with various treatises on alchemy, astrology, divination, and magic. It was thus judged not to be worthy of publication by the Polish Academy of Sciences and Letters in their projected *Corpus Philosophorum Medii Aevi*. Medieval scholars, however, had a higher opinion of the treatise, as is evident from the following facts.

Of the ninety codices known to contain the *De Pomo (The Apple)*, fifty-three are collections of primarily Aristotelian works; four are basically Arabic collections, while the others are either too miscellaneous in content or too incompletely described in *Aristoteles Latinus* to be thus classified.[23] In terms of Birkenmajer's classifications, the *De Pomo (The Apple)* is most frequently bound in with works of the first class, *i.e.* works which are extant in Greek and whose authenticity is certain. Thus, forty-two codices containing our treatise also include *De Bona Fortuna*,[24] *De Iuventute, De Longitudine,* and *De Sensu*. It is found with *De Somno* forty-one times, with *De Anima* forty, and thirty-nine times with *De Caelo, De Respiratione,* and *Metheora*. It is accompanied by *De Generatione* and *De Memoria* thirty-eight times, by *Physics* and *De Morte* thirty-six times, and *De Progressu Animalium* thirty-three times. The new translation of the *Metaphysics*, in fourteen books, is bound with the *De Pomo* thirty-two times, and the *De Motu Animalium* thirty-one. Because of discrepancies in titles, there may be some variations in these figures. But the general picture is certain enough: the medieval context of the *De Pomo (The Apple)* is the natural works of Aristotle.

Birkenmajer's second class consists of works which are certainly not by Aristotle but extant in Greek under his name;[25] among these we also find frequent companions of the *De Pomo (The Apple)*. *Physionomia* appears in forty-seven of our codices, immediately preceding the *De Pomo* in thirteen of them. *De Coloribus* appears thirty-eight times, *De Mundo* thirty-four, *De Lineis Indivisibilibus* also thirty-four, and *Epistola ad Alexandrum* thirty-two times. The schoolmen, then, frequently regarded the *De Pomo* as of equal authenticity with these other popular works.

---

[22] Alexandre Birkenmajer, *Classement des ouvrages attribués à Aristote par le moyen âge Latin* (Cracovie: Imprimerie de l'Université de Cracovie, 1932), pp. 10-18.

[23] Included in these figures is Kraemer's information about AL 802, as well as that from my own viewing of AL 34, AL 2050, AL 2185, and AL 2186.

[24] *De Bona Fortuna* is a compilation of Book II, chapter 8 of the *Magna Moralia* and Book VII, chapter 14 of the *Ethica Eudemia;* cf. *Aristoteles Latinus, pars prior,* p. 72.

[25] Birkenmajer, *Classement,* p. 10.

Of the two works in Birkenmajer's third class (non-authentic works which are extant only in medieval translations from the Greek but which are known to have circulated in Greece under Aristotle's name prior to the Christian era),[26] only one is coupled with our dialogue a significant number of times: the *De Inundatione Nili,* which is found in forty-two of the codices.

The botanical and mineralogical treatises which comprise Birkenmajer's sixth class are also well represented in these ninety codices: pseudo-Aristotelian writings translated from Arabic or Hebrew, but whose origin is in Greek or Byzantine sources.[27] Of these, the *De Proprietatibus Elementorum* (or *De Causis Proprietatum Elementorum*) appears in thirty-nine codices; *De Plantis* occurs thirty-six times, and *De Mineralibus* thrice.

The unique member of Birkenmajer's eighth class, the *Secretum Secretorum,* is bound with the *De Pomo (The Apple)* twenty times, immediately preceding it eight times and immediately following it in three others. The *De Regimine Sanitatis,* an extract from the *De Secretum Secretorum,* appears with the *De Pomo* twice.

From Birkenmajer's tenth class (works translated from the Arabic which were recognized as spurious by some medieval authors but accepted as authentic by others),[28] two form significant accompaniments to *The Apple:* the *Liber De Causis,* which appears in our codices forty times, and the *De Differentia Spiritus et Animae.*

A curious bit of confusion, probably due to the scribes' knowledge of *The Apple (De Pomo),* is evident in the manuscripts of the *Liber de Causis,* whose alternate title was gradually corrupted from "de puro bono" to "de puro aeterno" to "de primo cyterno" to "de pomo citrono." Thus, Bardenhewer reminds us of Jourdain's discovery that an old manuscript at Paris has at the end, in a later hand, "Expliciunt canones Aristotelis de puro aeterno . . . sive de causis."[29] He further notes that in a manuscript at the Bodleian Library, we can read, "Expliciunt canones Aristotelis de primo cyterno . . . sive de causis."[30] And finally,

[26] *Ibid.,* pp. 10-11.
[27] *Ibid.,* pp. 11-12. If further research should yield an ancient Greek original of the *De Pomo,* it would then be promoted from the ninth to the sixth of Birkenmajer's classes, and thus be publishable in *Corpus Philosophorum Medii Aevi.*
[28] Cf. Birkenmajer, *Classement,* pp. 10-11.
[29] Otto Bardenhewer, *Die pseudo-aristotelische Schrift Ueber das reine Gute bekannt unter dem Namen Liber de Causis* (Freiburg im B r e i s g a u:

Herder'sche Verlagshandlung, 1882), p. 56 and p. 140. This manuscript is apparently *AL* 565, of thirteenth century French provenance.
[30] Bardenhewer, *Die pseudo-Aristotelische . . . Liber de Causis,* p. 154, n. 3. He cites here Coxe's catalogue, which I have not seen, but which was also used by the editors of *AL.* The only codex in *AL* from this catalogue that contains the *De Causis* is #330, of fourteenth century Italian provenance.

AL 1488, a thirteenth-century English manuscript now at Naples, has an addition in a fifteenth-century hand which reads, "Expliciunt causationes Aristotelis de pomo citrono sive . . . de causis;" thus, eventually *Canones de puro bono (Canons on the Pure Good)* became *causationes de pomo citrono (Causes of the Fruit Citron)*, most likely through a confused awareness of *The Apple (De Pomo)*.[31]

The other work in this tenth class, the *De Differentia Spiritus et Animae*, whch, though written by Costa ben Luca, was included as a work of Aristotle's in many official guides to peripatetic philosophy, is in twenty-seven of the codices which include the *De Pomo*.

Finally, two short works which are also closely associated with our treatise in the manuscript tradition are placed by Birkenmajer in a special supplementary class. They are the *Liber de Vita Aristotelis*, which occurs forty-four times;[32] and the *De Intelligentia*, which is found thirty-nine times, thirty of them immediately following the *De Pomo*. In fact, the sequence *Vita Aristotelis, De Pomo, De Intelligentia* is frequent—and easy to understand: the supposed description of Aristotle's death makes a natural sequel to his supposed biography, and the *De Intelligentia*, containing the standard definitions of many scholastic terms, formed a convenient summary and glossary at the end of a codex.[33]

At least one, and possibly two, noted schoolmen are known to have commented on *The Apple* (H-L). One conjecture concerns Albert the Great, who refers several times to a work of his own entitled *De Immortalite Animae (On the Immortality of the Soul)*. At times this phrase seems to be a substitute title for one of his works which was also known as *De Natura Animae (On the Nature of the Soul)*.[34] It has been suggested, however, by P. G. Meerseman, that in other places the title may refer to a now lost work of Albert the Great which was a commentary on *The Apple*.[35] Another commentary, now extant in only one poorly legible manuscript, seems to have been done by Albert of Saxony, a master at Paris and Vienna who died in 1390.[36] Furthermore,

---

[31] I am grateful to Dr. John O. Riedl for calling this information to my attention.

[32] Cf. Birkenmajer, *Classement*, pp. 16-18. This anonymous *Life of Aristotle* was recently edited by Ingemar Düring in his *Aristotle in the Ancient Biographical Tradition* (Goteborg: Elanders Boktryckeri Aktiebolag, 1957), pp. 151-158. It is similar to two Greek lives, but its Greek source has perished. Its avid reception in Europe after its translation, sometime after 1230, can be seen from the fact that 65 manuscripts of it survive.

[33] Birkenmajer, *Classement*, p. 18.

[34] Bernhardus Geyer, (ed.), *Alberti Magni Liber de Natura et Origine Animae* (Monasterii Westfalorum in Aedibus Aschendorff, 1955), p. xvii.

[35] In his introduction to the *Opera Omnia B. Alberti Magni O.P.* (Brugis: Carolum Beyaert, 1931), p. 46.

[36] The manuscript, dated 1394, is Erfurt *Amplon. Qu.* 319; other manuscripts

Polish manuscripts of the fifteenth century are heavily annotated and glossed—another indication that the treatise was being carefully studied, at least in Cracow, in the fifteenth century.[37]

It is evident from the manuscript tradition, then, that the *Liber De Pomo sive De Morte Aristotilis, (The Apple, or Aristotle's Death)*, though not on the well-known official lists in the medieval manuals of instruction, was widely taught in universities all over Europe; in fact, we can say that it was at least informally considered part of the standard collection of Aristotelian writings. After its translation into Latin in the second half of the thirteenth century, it spread rapidly; it was copied in increasing numbers in the fourteenth century, and maintained its popularity in the fifteenth. This fact is significant for our understanding of the attitude of educated men toward Aristotle. That this blatant attempt to posthumously Christianize Aristotle could find such a ready audience, and this after the wide dissemination of his *Metaphysics* and *De Anima* in the schools, and the achievements of Thomas Aquinas and others in recognizing that the *Liber de Causis,* for example, was spurious—this fact shows us how slow and precarious, indeed, is the progress of human thought. Unless those few who achieve real progress find disciples equal to the task of transmission, their achievement is easily lost. The decline of scholasticism has at least part of its explanation here.

As a concluding postscript, it is interesting to note a few traces of the *De Pomo* in medieval and renaissance vernacular writings from various parts of Europe, as indications of its acceptance beyond the circle of formal instruction. In 1387, we find it mentioned by John of Trevisa, the English poet who translated the *Polychronicon* of Radulphus Higden from Latin into English. Outraged by Higden's repetition of the story transmitted by Gregory of Nazianzen that Aristotle committed suicide, Trevisa asks why Higden did not instead cite *The Apple* for the true story of the philosopher's death:

Why telled he nought how it is iwrite in de book of the

in the same codex are Aristotelian commentaries by Albert of Saxony. Cf. Plezia, *Liber de Pomo*, p. 11.

For a time, it was erroneously thought that another commentary existed in Erfurt *Amplon. Oct.* 80, folios 31-40, but Plezia has examined the manuscript and seen that this is not the case. Cambridge manuscript 1525c was also once thought to contain a commentary by Albert the Great on *The Apple,* but does not. See Plezia, *Liber de*

Pomo, pp. 11-12 for correction of these earlier opinions.

Renan's statement that Averroes wrote a great commentary on *The Apple* which is mentioned in "the list of the Escorial" is now recognized as false. Cf. Ernest Renan, *Averroès et l'Averroisme* (Paris: Auguste Durand, 1852), p. 48. Steinschneider, *H. Ü.* p. 267, says that this statement rests on a false reading.

[37] Plezia, *Liber de Pomo*, p. 14.

appel (how Aristotel deyde and hylde an appel) in his hond (and hadhe) comfort of de smyl, and taughte his scoleres how dey schulde lyve and come to God, and be wid God wid outen ende. And at the laste his hond gan to quake, and the appel fil doun of his hond, and his face wax al wan, and so Aristotil ghelde up the goost and deyde.[38]

The Apple was also known at this time among the French; reference to it appears at the beginning of the poem *Respit de la mort* by Jean Lefèbre:

> Aristote, le bien sage homme,
> ou petit livret de la pomme
> qu'il tenoit au lit de sa mort . . .
> ("Aristotle, the truly wise man, in the
> little book about the apple which he held
> on his death-bed. . . .")[39]

In the next century, an Italian Jew, Gedalja ben Joseph, in his *Chain of Tradition,* mentions both *The Book of the Apple* and *The Book of the Golden House* as falsely ascribed to Aristotle—an apparent echo of Maimonides.[40] Finally, an Italian renaissance writer, Caelius Rhodiginus (who died in 1520), mentions the *De Pomo* twice in his *Lectures;* he used the work as a source for Greek beliefs on immortality, but refers to it as being of unknown authorship. His words are:

> I have seen it reported—in a book of unknown authorship—that Aristotle's life was prolonged for a while by the fragrance of an apple from which the book takes its title.[41]

Such, then, is the story of the manuscript tradition of the Latin translation of *The Apple.* First produced by Manfred, who found comfort from it during a serious illness, the treatise was rapidly copied and spread throughout Europe, probably through Manfred's donation to the University of Paris in 1263. The work became even more popular in the next century, and found its way in many instances into the corpus of works that were accepted by the schoolmen as genuinely Aristotle's. It was welcomed as evidence that Aristotle was converted

[38] Rev. Joseph Rawnon Lumby (ed.), *Polychronicon Ranulphi Higden Monachi Cestrensis, together with the English Translations of John Trevisa and of an Unknown Writer of the Fifteenth Century* (London: Longman and Co., 1871), p. 371. This is volume 41 of *Rerum Britannicarum Medii Aevi Scriptores,* or *The Chronicles and Memorials of Great Britain and Ireland during the Middle Ages.* This reference to Trevisa comes from Hertz, "Das Buch vom Apfel," pp. 378-79.

[39] From Lecoy, "Sur la date du *Mors de la pomme,*" *Romania* LXXIV (1953), p. 509, cited by Plezia, *Liber de Pomo,* p. 15.

[40] Hertz, "Das Buch vom Apfel," p. 379.

[41] My translation of the Latin quoted by Hertz, "Das Buch vom Apfel," pp. 379-80 and Plezia, *Liber de Pomo,* p. 15. There is apparently no modern edition of this work.

to Christian ideas, and all of this despite the absurdity of attributing its doctrine to the same man who wrote the *Metaphysics* and *De Anima*. Nor was its popularity confined to students of philosophy, for we also find traces of it in the vernacular literatures of three different countries in the late Middle Ages and early Renaissance. Today it survives in almost a hundred manuscripts. We are happy to make it available now to English-speaking students of the history of thought.

The Apple, or Aristotle's Death

PROLOGUE

Since man was made, of all creatures, the most worthy image in the likeness of God, and since the noble was created for the sake of the ignoble, nothing should be considered more excellent in him than that he should know himself and his Creator; nothing is more contemptible than that, given over entirely to sensible things, he should remain ignorant of both. For granted that he can receive enlightenment in respect to the former and to the latter from the First, Who enlightens every man coming into this world[1] and has signed us with the light of His own countenance,[2] so that he can attain to God, the fount of true light, his end (like the sun, which rises and sets and returns to its own place)[3]; nevertheless, he is so greatly impeded by the darkness of the companion subjected to him, from which every weakness of his corruption originates, that he is deformed by the vice of earthly desire and, like a beast of burden, understands nothing. And since the memory of his special dignity is too confused to allow a more worthy determination of his choice, wandering instead in a cloud of ignorance, he fails to attain the term of ultimate perfection to which his right inclination was leading him. For according to his knowledge or ignorance, a man is either close to God or far from Him. Hence may he who is freed from the deviation of such error, and is led away from the palpable density of the body's darkness, find the way of life from which he had miserably strayed; may he bring his eyes, so accustomed to darkness, to the light of manifest truth. It profits him to be illuminated by the splendors of human teaching, by which he might know the sublimity of the Most High and the Maker of the universe, might turn to Him with continuous attention, and might know himself to be both noble and ignoble. By these may he also restrain his vices, so that by transcending the powers of the body by the aid of the sciences, and by the attaining of virtues, he may become like his own Source and continually enjoy the solace of eternity.

Indeed, for many the path of life would be impassable if the wise did not diminish the vices of men by their teachings; if they did not light the lamp of truth for those who are thus imprisoned in a body, and if, holding themselves up as an example of the rejection of mortal things (in which there is no permanence), they did not lead to the honor and fear of God those many others among men who, seeking

---

[1] Cf. *John*, 1, 9. All identifications of Scriptural allusions are from Plezia's notes.

[2] *Psalm* 4, 7.

[3] *Ecclesiastes* 1, 5.

pleasures so licentiously, differ not at all from the beasts. But striving for virtue, they have learned to correct the lewdness of the body by self-control; so that they may not be afraid to die; and raised above the rewards of the world and well sustained by the special gift of proven security and of indubitable felicity, may hasten with all eagerness to the fulfillment of their desires.

Wherefore we, Manfred, son of the divine and august emperor Frederick, by the grace of God prince of Taranto, lord of the mountain of honor, Sant Angelo, and governor[4]-general of the illustrious Conrad, the second king of Sicily, were laid low by the misfortunes of human infirmity, the result of a discord of the concordant elements of which we, like others, are constituted. When a grave illness weakened our body to the point that no one thought we could continue to live in the flesh, great anxiety tortured those present, since they thought that we were frightened at the imminence of our death. But a group of venerable teachers at the court of the imperial, divine, august, and most serene emperor, our lord and father, had presented theological and philosophical documents about the nature of the world, the flux of bodies, the creation of souls, their eternity and perfection, and the instability of material things and the stability of forms, which are not affected by disaster or deficiency in their matter. Bearing these teachings firmly in mind, we were not so saddened at our dissolution as they thought, even though we could not in justice rely on our own merits for possessing the perfection which is our reward, but solely on the Creator's mercy.

Among these was a book called *The Apple*, produced by Aristotle, the prince of philosophers, at the end of his life. In it he shows that wise men do not sorrow over the death of their vile lodging, but joyfully run to the reward of perfection; for its sake they did not hesitate in the least to spend their time and their life in the supreme labors of studies, inwardly fleeing the hindrances of the world. We told those present that they should read this book, since from it they would gather that this kind of passing away is of little moment. Since this book was not to be found among Christians, and since we read it in Hebrew, translated from the Arabic into Hebrew; once our health had been restored, we translated it from the Hebrew tongue into Latin, for the instruction of many. In it certain remarks by a compiler have been included. For Aristotle did not write the book, but it is extant as written

[4] "Governor" is my inadequate translation of the term *baiulus*, a technical name in Frederick's constitution for fourth-rank officials of varied duties in both the financial and judicial branches of his government. Cf. Luigi Salvatorelli, *A Concise History of Italy* (New York: Oxford University Press, 1940), p. 228.

by others—those who wished to find out the cause of his joy at his death, as is contained in detail in the book.

[The Apple]

When the way of truth had been closed to the wise and the way of right understanding was blocked, some wise men came together into one house and, with one heart, tried to explain and understand the path of rectitude, by which men should be able to live. They found no path except one, which was that a man should wish for his neighbor what he wishes for himself; that he should withdraw himself from shameful behavior, confess the truth, inflict judgment upon himself, and fear his Creator.

There was at that time a wise man, great, famous and intelligent, whose name was Aristotle. All the wise men of his time used to listen to his learning and understand what he meant, and were taught by him. When he was near death from a fatal illness[5] all the wise men assembled and went to see him to investigate the causes of his infirmity. They found him holding an apple in his hand and smelling it. He had gotten very thin, on account of the severity of his illness, and was in his last agony.

When they saw him, they were very upset and came close to him; as they approached him, they found that his face was bright and he himself was cheerful; and he greeted them first.

Then they said to him, "O our lord and master! When we first saw you, our spirit left us and we were disturbed because we saw a violent illness in you and your strength greatly weakened. And then when we saw you happy and your face bright, our spirit, which had departed, returned."

Aristotle in fact joked with them, saying "Do not think in your hearts that I am happy because I hope to escape from the severe illness which I have; for I know well that I am about to die, and cannot escape, because the pain has greatly increased. And if it weren't for this apple which I am holding in my hand and whose odor strengthens me and prolongs my life a little while, I would have already expired.

"But the sensible soul, which we share with the beasts, is sustained by a good odor. And I am happy that I am departing from this world, which is composed of contraries; for the four elements, from which every created thing under the sun is made, are contraries. One is cold, another hot, another dry, another moist. How can a body composed of such elements last, or be prolonged in life, except briefly? When those elements are in equilibrium and do not oppose each

---

[5] 4 Kings, 13, 14. My rather free translation has obscured the verbal similarity of the Latin text to this passage from the Bible.

other, and when no one of them overcomes its contrary—then one's life is well-ordered, and he can live. But when one dominates another, diminishes and weakens its own contrary, then illness comes. If some highly skilled doctor can be found, who recognizes the illness, so that he can strengthen the weak elements and weaken the stronger, then the body is restored to its strength and can convalesce. But many of them neither know nor recognize the case; they increase the body's illness and cause it to descend to ruin and death.

"The intelligible soul indeed has souls under it and rules them; it is not composite, but is of one simple element. This is the intellectual soul, which discerns between good and evil, understands that all lines which are equal to another line are equal to each other, and knows that three is an odd number and four is even. This soul among the mortal animals, found only in men, knows its Creator and understands itself. Another soul, the memorative, makes a man remember things he has forgotten. A third soul shows a man in his mind whatever is hidden from his presence at the time, as when someone in one city imagines himself in another. This soul sees dreams and many things which are portents of the future. A fourth soul invents such arts as weaving, spinning, and the like. And if time were not too short for conversing longer about these matters, I would show you what each of those souls is in itself, its uses, and whatever is necessary for each."

One of the wise men standing near, named Symas, answered him, saying, "Our lord and master, you have always treated us well and taught us many sciences. Now do us a favor, and strengthen our hearts just as you have strengthened your own, so that we might learn not to fear the day of death and may not be upset, as other men are. They are disturbed by death, as we see of those who are dying, who pass away in great fear and perturbation because they do not know where they are going or what hope they will have. Then you shall do us two favors: one, you shall give us a teaching by which our hearts will be strengthened; and the other, you will quiet our doubts about you and our grief at your departure, since your end will be peace and perpetual rest."

Aristotle replied to him, "Behold, I will teach and guide you so that you will understand and be convinced of the truth of my words. Although this would be a great labor for me, I will keep sniffing the fragrance of this apple in order to restore my spirits to me, until I finish my discourse. Because I know that thence I shall have a good reward, for you will understand this matter, an accomplishment which will not be vain."

Then each of the disciples rose and kissed the master's head. He said to them, "First I will ask if you profess and believe in philosophy, which contains all sciences, that it is true, that he who studies it investigates truth and rectitude in their most high, divine degrees? And in philosophy is found the difference between man and the other animals?"

They said, "Whether we like it or not, we confess this to be so."

He said, "If this is true, then the good which comes to a man from the sciences and the great progress which he makes through them either come to him in this world, in which we are today, or after death, in another world. If you say in this world, in which we are before we die, then you have not allowed the right value to knowledge. For very many foolish men, who did not walk along the path of rectitude and did not recognize their Creator, have finished their days in good fortune and their years in the fulfillment of their desires; and there are many wise men who abounded in the sciences and understanding, who acquired learning, recognized their Creator, and yet who suffer the privation of good fortune and of peace. And you, if you are disturbed and afraid of death, which is the departure of the soul from the unknowing body and its entrance into comprehension of the divine degrees and union with wise and happy souls—you do not allow knowledge its proper rank or value; you are submerged in a bestial spirit along with the other beasts."

Then Aristotle said, "Moreover, I will ask you another question. Do you know that death is nothing else but the departure of the soul from the body?"

They said, "Yes."

He said to them, "Are the rest of you happy about learning science and sad when you cannot learn about it or understand it?"

They said, "Yes."

He said to them, "If that is the case, then you already see that the unknowing body neither sees nor hears nor understands anything except by the power of the soul, conjoined with it in its own existence. And the body, enjoying eating and drinking and other pleasures, is opposed to the soul's ascent to its proper dignity. When it departs from the body, it departs from that which is contrary to its good and to fulfillment of its desire.

"I have already shown you that a man cannot comprehend the noble sciences except through the stages of the soul, when it is purged, perfected, and cleansed of its impurities; when it departs from the uncleanness which is imprisoned with it—which is produced out of earth, and pursues the pleasures of eating, drinking, and amusements, as do the other animals, which lack the wise soul that makes a man restrain his impulses and desires. Because through these stages a man rises above his equal when he dominates his passions and restrains his nature, out of horror at the delights of the body, which defile him; when he seeks instead the delights of the soul in learning the sciences of God, Who created His world by His own wisdom; and when he investigates His ways and understands His secrets. Then the eyes of his soul are opened, they greatly rejoice, and they are delighted by a pleasure which is different from bodily pleasures. For all the allurements of the body are limited; they end in nothing, destroy its substance, and cause it to descend to death. But the delights of the soul are to understand its Creator, to consider His wisdom in the works of the heavens, the courses of the spheres, their forms, and the fact that all things are established and rooted in wisdom. And if he is not able to comprehend profundities of this kind, let a man look at himself and the subtlety of his members, each one of the muscles serving to move him, drawing his body to rest and to motion; and powers located in each member for the service of the body, in which nothing is defective or superfluous. Through this he can recognize his Creator and will know that the study of man as he is in this life is despicable; but a soul which desires to know those other sciences is perfect and upright. This soul is not saddened or disturbed when it departs from the body, which opposes the fulfillment of its desire and its quest.

"Furthermore, do you not know that a pure and perfect philosopher mortifies all his desires in this world, for eating, drinking, dress, and other pleasures, for treasures of gold and silver? That he despises all pleasures which lead to the destruction of both body and soul? For he who is deeply intent upon eating and drinking, and uses the least pleasures of this kind (which he can enjoy only while he is eating) corrupts his body with diseases and pain. For the nascent humors in the body, which are the source of a man's life and strength, increase immoderately as a result of much food and drink. One is blood, the source of life; it is warm and moist. The second is black bile, which is cold and dry. The third is yellow bile, which is warm and dry. The fourth is phlegm, which is cold and moist. Each of these is diminished and increased and alters its nature as a result of excessive and variable eating. Likewise, one who makes great use of venereal pleasure ages his body and macerates its substance. A wise man is careful. He despises all such things and perfects his soul by seeking knowledge of his Creator, Who made being itself out of nothing. He is the man who should rejoice at death, which is the departure of the soul from the body. For what profit would he have in life, since he has mortified all pleasures, which are despicable and vile? Rather, he ought to exult at the time when his soul approaches its Creator and rejoice in His splendor. It should not fear to come near Him. Nor will it find anyone to oppose or repulse it, as will those souls who pursued vanities and did not strive for knowledge nor rectify their ways. And these are the ones who can neither approach to nor arrive at that place; they find one to oppose and repulse them. And the rest of you—if you are wise and intelligent, as you say, and have hated all the pleasures of the body, as you are bound to do along the way of the sciences—why are you disturbed or afraid? If you have taken the root, then delight in the fruit."

Symas replied, "O our lord and master! You have turned us into great lovers of death, which before we had greatly feared."

And after him, one of the disciples called Melion responded, "Up until this moment I was very much afraid of death, but now I am saddened and terrified by the length of life."

Cariton answered and said to him, "Why are you saddened and terrified of life and length of days? For if you aspire to death or seek it out, you shall find it; nor will you find anyone to oppose you."

Melion answered him, "That is not the reply of a prudent man, such as you are, because even though I am not afraid of death, nevertheless I do not seek it before it comes. For a man's profit in life is to reach the highest rank and learn the sciences and aim at the paths of philosophy. For through it he shall study his Creator, until he comes through his knowledge to the First Workman, Who made being out of nothing, Who is the Beginner of all Beginnings and the Origin of all Origins; and he shall know that the world cannot withstand Him. An ignorant soul does not recognize Him. By His knowledge He set up the spheres, and in each sphere the shining stars, and gave them the power of ruling over this lower world, of causing good and evil, death and life, riches and poverty. All this they do by the power of the Ruler who orders things rightly. Those who look at the stars and consider their dominion over this world attribute power and dominion to the stars, make them a god, and serve and praise them. They think that all the things which they do, they do of their very selves and by their own power, and that they rule by their own force. And in this the ancient wise men were deceived, for they made many images of the stars, which they used to serve, and they forgot about their Source. And each man adopted for himself one of the stars, whichever he wished—some the sun, some the moon, some others. But if it had been as these wise men thought, the actions of the stars and their courses would always be the same. But they do not change their directions and proceed, by a power given them, to do their own pleasures and desires. In rising and setting, they do not move now from east to west and now from west to east, setting their pace according to their own

[54]

will, without any opposition; because all the stars are like a servant, who has one task only, and who does not have the power to vary or modify it. Their motion and course is not from themselves nor by their own power, because the higher sphere is the one which makes all things move. This power was established in the first sphere according to the order of the Creator.[6] All of this is shown in the book of philosophy, in which all the sciences are detailed and their foundations explained.

"At first[7] all men were in error in this matter, until the coming of Noe, who was the first to recognize the Creator of the spheres; and he knew that each thing and the source itself had a science and a greater rank, the high and the highest.[8] And after Noe, was born

[6] The Latin author contradicts himself here: he says that the wise men thought the stars were divine; but if this were so, they would move in an unvarying pattern. He then surprisingly says that the stars *do* move in an unvarying pattern, and are therefore *not* divine.

According to Plezia's note, *Liber De Pomo*, p. 67, this passage is so defective in the Latin as to show that the translator misunderstood the Hebrew and perverted its meaning. The sense of the Hebrew is that the ancients failed to recognize the regularity of stellar motion, which they would have seen as proof that the stars are not self-directed and hence not divine. Isidor Kalisch's translation reads: "These men had not the understanding that the effort and course of the stars are always fixed and happen in an invariable manner, that their order is not changed, and that they cannot deviate from their innate laws; they must rather move according to the power granted them, and that a strong will leads them from East to West and from West to East without opposition. The stars obey the will like slaves; nor are they at liberty to decline or deviate from their course. Their motion and course do not originate in a free power which is determined in them; but the higher sphere is their guide and leader. In this highest sphere was but the power of God . . . ." *Ha-Tapuach*, pp. 23-24.

I have given a strictly literal translation of the Latin as it stands in Plezia's text. The sense is obscure because pluperfect subjunctives, indicating the protasis of a contrary-to-fact conditional, are followed by unexpected present indicatives: "Et si hoc *fuisset*, ut isti sapientes intellexerunt aut cognoverunt, *oporteret,* quod opera stellarum et cursus earum semper essent uno modo tantum, nec *mutant* imperata et *incedunt* secundum virtutem ipsis datam ad faciendum voluptates earum in ascendendo et descendendo nunc de oriente ad occidens nunc de occidente ad oriens *mouentur* secundum uoluntatem suam sine contradictore." (My italics). It is impossible to tell whether *nec* governs one, two or all three of the verbs following it.

The argument in the Hebrew that the stars are not divine, as is shown by the regularity of their motion, is the reverse of Aristotle's authentic view. He sees unvarying circular motion as a proof of divinity.

[7] These three paragraphs are rightly identified by Plezia and others as an interpolation by the Hebrew translator. Theories based on this passage which attribute *The Apple* to a Jewish author are thus groundless. There is, however, nothing in the Arabic version which would preclude Jewish authorship except for the brief reference to Hermes, which could easily be another interpolation. See above, p. 35.

[8] Plezia's note, *Liber De Pomo*, p. 67, explains that this sentence also dis-

Abraham, who was wiser than all and gained much knowledge, and perceived that his whole generation was wandering in error. And when God commanded him to sacrifice his only son, he was willing to do it, because he had been made perfect in the service of God. He knew that the sun and moon and stars have a First Mover; and he did not follow the way of his father, who adored idols of the goddesses in Haran. These were idols of the moon; his whole generation sacrificed to those idols and served them; and flames subjected their sons and daughters to them.[9]

"It is fitting that a man such as he, who arrives at that perfection and is learned in the way of philosophy, should seek death, as you say. But I have not yet reached that high level; wherefore I do not seek death, until it shall come, because I cannot, in a short time, arrive at that science and a high perfection of this kind."

Aristotle replied to Cariton, "The answer of Melon [sic] seems right to me, and his words have pleased us greatly; he has spoken the truth, and I acknowledge his statements and praise his meaning."

Then a disciple by the name of Arastaratus said, "Our master, add more to your friendship for us: tell us how we may learn philosophy, which has that great dignity, which draws a man away from the obscurity of ignorance and the darkness of folly to the clarity of knowledge and the light of understanding."

Aristotle answered, "He who wishes to learn philosophy and to

torts the meaning of the Hebrew, which is that there is an absolute, highest principle of all things, in which supreme power resides, and by whose power all things move. Kalisch's English reads, "He comprehended, that there must be a first beginning and a supreme leader to and of everything, in whom the greatest wisdom and all sublime and excellent properties are innate." *Ha-Tapuach*, p. 24.

[9] This last phrase reads, "et filios et filias subiciebant sibi ignis," which I have translated literally as it stands. Plezia's note, *Liber De Pomo*, p. 68, explains that the Latin author has nodded again; the sense of the Hebrew is that they led their children through flames. In the English of Isidor Kalisch we read: "to whom the people sacrificed their children as burnt offerings. . . ." *Ha-Tapuach*, p. 25. The Latin scribes,

recognizing a defective sentence, tried various ways of correcting it: e.g. by omitting *ignis* or changing it to *ignibus*, or by substituting *sacrificabant ignibus* for *subiciebant sibi ignis*.

In addition, an interesting Old French gloss has crept into the text at this point, "*et comme le même Goulias.*" Plezia takes this as a reference to the bishop Golias, a legendary figure who gave his name to the Goliards, who were solemnly condemned in synods in the years 1227, 1231, 1232, and 1239. Cf. *Liber de Pomo*, p. 68, where Plezia correctly cites F. J. de Ghellinck, *L'essor de la littérature latine au XII siècle* (Bruxelles-Bruges—Paris, 1955), second edition, p. 505. The gloss is included in the printed edition of 1496, *GKW* 2341, but not in Plezia's text.

be wise should read the first eight books which I have written,[10] until he comes to the book *On The Soul*. From it he will know where in the body is the seat of the soul, and its nature; if it is imprisoned in it, or if it exists before it is in it, or is created with the body; if it stays in it, or if it will arise and be revived from the dead; why it is concealed from the eyes of all the living after it departs from the body, or if it dies with it.[11] When he shall consider these things that happen to the soul, then he will know his Creator and walk in the right path; he shall not turn aside to the right or to the left. This is the greatest perfection; there is no higher.

"Now I have shown you the way of truth; and I have not departed from the right path, for those who teach and give instruction ought not to lie or falsify their words. Every man who restrains the desires of the body and furnishes his soul with the doctrine of philosophy and knows the degrees—when he departs from the body, when death comes upon him, if he shall be afraid or disturbed, it will be a sign that his knowledge is not perfect. For he has not attained the purpose of the science of philosophy, and all those who hear of this will despise him. But he who clings to the way of the wise, afflicts his soul, restrains his nature, trusts his Creator, renounces evil, chooses good, and is not terrified of death—he it is who ought to be called a wise man. He should be said to have attained the purpose of philosophy— not indeed one who knows the way of the science and yet is disturbed about death, when his soul departs from his body. For what use is knowledge without its fruit?

"For this reason, philosophy ought to be proclaimed, in order to teach the ignorant those things which they have not understood from the sciences and from instruction; for they have not recognized their Creator. Their knowing does not include good or evil; they are ignorant except of what they learned about good and evil as children. If someone offers them instruction about a good life, they accept it, and it remains fixed in their soul; it is not weakened or altered. But the same thing happens if someone teaches them a way that is not right. Between these and one who keeps to the right path there is a great difference. The first ones whom we mentioned, although they are on a good path, are like beasts. There is no difference between them and the beasts which are led along the right path by the man who bridles them. These are men who do not know how to think for themselves.

---

[10] This phrase refers to the logical works, not the *Physics*, as the subsequent summary of contents shows. It was usual for the Syrians and Arabs to refer to Aristotle's logical works as simply "The Eight Books," following a grouping which dates back to Simplicius. Cf. Nicholas Rescher, *Studies in Arabic Logic* (Pittsburgh: University of Pittsburgh Press, 1963), pp. 30-31.
[11] cf. above, p. 25, n. 66.

"There is another kind of men, whose perception and understandnig are ready and capable of all things; they grasp all things with their own minds. Of these there are two sects: the first of them say that the world has no beginning or end, and that there is nothing new under the sun; that one generation passes away and another comes,[12] but the earth remains forever and has neither Sustainer nor Ruler. These deny the Root. And there are others, understanding by nature, who say that the soul is created simultaneously with the body, or made out of the body; and as long as its body exists, the soul too exists, in its being. They find proof of this in the case of a boy, who as long as he is little and of tender age does not take in the sciences nor possess understanding, because his body is soft and moist and has not attained its strength. If it were true that the soul was of another creation than the body, why would the body impede the soul from understanding? Especially since when the body is sick, the soul is weakened and made foolish; so that, as a result of the infirmity of the body, it thinks and speaks differently, and its understanding is diminished. These men look for and apprehend the great science of God and His works in the members of the body, in its essence and sinews.

"I have already made opinions of this kind clear in the books I have written; I have demonstrated their impossibilities and demolished them according to the way of the truth of science."

The scholars standing near said to him, "Our lord and master, teach us which is the right science that a man ought to learn and understand, and how he ascends through it to the high level of the science of rectitude."

Aristotle replied, "None of the sciences is like philosophy, which enlightens the soul and makes her delight in this world in perfection and rectitude; these are the foundation of her well-being. Through it, she can perceive and understand the good of the other world; and one who learns it, finds life in both worlds. For in the first eight books are found all the ways of science, by which a man can comprehend and possess the principles for all methods. He can know the arguments adduced concerning them: which ones rightly apply to disputable matters and which ones separate him from those not possessing the right way. Through this something of the truth may be known. For arguments of this kind are in the vicinity of truth; yet, they are not true. Nor are they of any use, except that through them one who speaks from his own knowledge can acquire courage. He can weaken the words of his opponent and overcome his discourse by the force of his own knowledge, with arguments that are well-ordered and admir-

[12] *Eccl.* 1, 10 and 1, 4.

able, so that his opponent will have no power to resist. This science is useful in the same way as the scorpion is useful as an antidote: although it is a poison, yet if given to one who is ill it lessens his pain and provides a remedy.[13] A philosopher should know all arguments of this kind, so that he will not be deceived by sophistry nor taken in by words, but will understand the topics and propositions in which a sophism appears. In these books is the truth of all the sciences, but not their particulars.

"I have written another book, called *Metaphysics;* in it I have shown clearly that the upper firmament and the stars are not of the elements which we see existing under the moon; they are of another nature, which we have neither power nor strength to understand. And there, from on high, the wise soul flowed into the body; it is not composed of another element, but on the contrary is simple, clean, and pure. Blessed is that soul which is not corrupted by the evil works of this world, and knows its Creator! It will return to its own place in great delights—not with the pleasures of the body, which have been despised. And woe to the sinful soul, which has no virtue nor power to return to its own place! It is not able to ascend to its homeland, because the shameful deeds of corporeal pleasure impede its ascent on high."

When the wise man had approached the end of his discourse, his hands began to tremble, and the apple which he was holding fell from them. And when his face had begun to turn black, he expired. One by one the scholars fell forward over him, kissed him, and raised a lament together, wailing a great wail. They said, "May He Who gathers the souls of philosophers gather your soul and place it again among His treasures, as is fitting for the soul of a man upright and perfect, as you are."

---

[13] This reference to the scorpion echoes a remark first made by Ammonius and then handed down in a continuous tradition; the gist of it is that Aristotle in his logical works acts like a wise physician in that he gives poison in order to cure. Cf. Düring, *Aristotle in the Ancient Biographical Tradition*, p. 447.

Appendix

The Book of the Apple

(Translated from the Persian by D. S. Margoliouth. Reprinted from the *Journal of the Royal Asiatic Society of Great Britain and Ireland*.)

This is the translation of a discourse which Aristotle delivered at the time of his death. It is said that when the life of the sage Aristotle approached its end, some of his disciples came to see him. When they saw the emaciation of his frame, and his weakness, and perceived about him the signs of death, they despaired of his life; only the joy, alacrity, and clearness of intellect that they perceived in him showed them that he took a different view of his condition from that which was taken by others. Then one of the disciples said to him: Our grief over you is greater than your grief over yourself, and we are more vexed than you concerning your departure; if it be that you feel otherwise than we feel about you, tell us also of this.—Aristotle said: The joy that you perceive in me does not arise from my cherishing any desire for life, but from my confidence about my condition after death.—A disciple named Simmias said: If you have this confidence, it were better that you should explain the ground of it to us also, that we may be as certain as you.—Aristotle said: Although it is difficult for me to talk, still for your sake I will endure some trouble: but first let me hear Kriton, for I can see that he wishes to say something.— Kriton said: Although I should much like to hear your conversation, and acquire knowledge thereby, O teacher of mankind, the physician whom you employ commanded me not to induce you to talk, on the ground that talking would make you warm, and should the heat get the better of you the cure would be delayed, and the effect of the drugs impeded.—Aristotle said: I will disobey the advice of the physician, and will employ no drug but the scent of an apple; which will keep me alive till I have given you the lecture to which you have a right. Why should I not speak, when the best thing I hope to obtain from the drugs is the power to speak? Come now, tell me, Do you grant the excellence of wisdom or not? They answered: Our only reason for honouring wisdom is the fact that we know it to excel other things.—Aristotle said: Is its excellence in this world or in the next? —They said: We do not deny the excellence of wisdom, and necessity forces us to place its excellence and value in the next world. Aristotle: Then why do you abhor death and adhere to the notion that some detriment will accrue to you therefrom, when you ought to perceive that death, horrible as it is to the vulgar, is nevertheless nothing but the freeing of the soul from its bodily case?—Disc.: How so? Let us know more.—Aristotle: Does the knowledge which you have acquired make you glad or not? And does the knowledge which has escaped you make you sorry or not?—Disc.: The former is true in both cases.—Aristotle: Through which then do you acquire knowledge— through the body, which is a blind, deaf, impotent, and useless mass when the spirit departs from it, or by the spirit whereby a man is continually rendered capable of learning, seeing, knowing and speaking, so long as it is with him?—Disc.: Doubtless through the vitality and goodness of the spirit knowledge is acquired, and by the dullness of the body it is kept out of it.—Aristotle: Since then it is clear that knowledge is a product of the spirit, and that the dullness of the body keeps it out, and that by the acquisition of knowledge you become glad, whereas by being precluded from it you become sorry, evidently you must prefer the separation of the spirit from the body to the persistence of the spirit in the body; and separation from the body must be better for the spirit than abiding in the body. Do you not see that the desires and delights of the body such as women and children and wealth and eating and drinking still more impede the search after wisdom? and that when you abandon those lusts you do so in order to protect the intellect and to devote yourselves to knowledge?—Disc.: Certainly.—Aristotle.—Then, since you confess that lusts have the power to damage the intellect, surely the body which enjoys those lusts must be more detrimental to the intellect?—Disc.: Our judgment forces us to agree with what your discourse has proved thus far; but what shall we do and how shall we act, in order to become as brave about death as you are, and as regardless of life as you are?—Aristotle: The best means for a seeker of knowledge to attain his end is an effort on the part of the speaker to speak only what is true, and of the hearer to hear correctly. I will now endeavour to speak truly; do you endeavour on your part to hear and receive correctly and truly. Do you not know that the meaning of the word 'philosophy' is 'fondness for wisdom'? and that the mind in its substance and origin is philosophy, and only delights in it, and only obtains peace therefrom?—Disc.: Certainly.—Aristotle: Do you not know that wisdom is the joy of the mind, and that wisdom can be obtained by goodness of soul and mind: now goodness of soul consists in its adjustment, and the adjustment of the mind consists in diminution of phlegm, rheum and blood?—Disc.:Aye.—Aristotle: If the goodness of the mind lie in its adjustment, and its adjustment in the diminution of those humours, when those humours altogether depart, it will become sounder and better?—Disc.: We cannot fail to admit the truth of what you say, but nevertheless we do not find in ourselves the same pleasure in death that we perceive in you.—Aristotle: Since sight guides the seer to his gain and preserves him from harm, try to let me increase your sight as to the advantage of death. O friends of wisdom! do you not see that the seeker after wisdom whose soul has become free from sin has mortified himself before death in respect of friends, and wealth, and empire, for the sake of which men desire the life of this world, and undertaken much sorrow and a heavy burden in seeking wisdom—sorrow so great that it can only be relieved by death? What desire has he for life who enjoys none of the pleasures of life: and why need he flee from death who can only rest in death? Nay! He does wrong, whosoever seeks the name of philosophy without being worthy of its meaning: and he is ignorant who fancies that in the comforts, pleasures and delights of this world the road to philosophy can be found. Can you desire that the name of knowledge should be bestowed on you whilst you are enjoying the pleasures of this world, of eating, drinking, and so on?—Disc.: We have no such desire, nor do we seek any such thing. How could we aspire to be philosophers while caring for this world, when we have seen that whenever there has been any excess in food or drink, or there manifests itself in the heart any motion of something contrary to the intellect, such as lust, or anger, or covetousness, or envy, the intellect remains inactive all that time; whereas, if that motion come not into play, then the blood only is at work, and there is nothing which serves better to protect it, and from which protection is more sought than the intellect.— Aristotle: The branch of a thing does not come but of the root, and the part is not but of the whole. If ye abstain in this world from lusts, but are attached to this world in your heart, your abstinence is not perfect. Now the root of attachment to the world lies in love of self-preservation. Hence every one who abstains from its lusts, but desires to remain in the world has caught the branch and neglected the root; whereas he is perfect and has reached the goal who has both root and branch.—Simmias: I have been abstemious in regard to the pleasures of this world; but now from what I have heard you say, I am anxious to remain in it no longer. Should that not be granted me, at least I shall endeavour to walk in your footsteps, and adopt your way of life, O teacher of mankind!—Kriton: My mind's eye now shows me that there is no one to whom death is not detrimental except the philosopher. Whosoever has attained thereunto and become perfect, let him seek death and desire it; but whoso has failed to attain thereto, let him flee from death his farthest, and avoid it his hardest. For nothing but wisdom withstands death and gives peace from its pain.—Zeno said: Aristotle's discourse leaves us no right to participate in pleasure or to endeavour to remain in the world, and the fact that he is more courageous about death than I—though I do not fear it very much— comes from his having been at greater pains than I to set his affairs right; had I looked after myself as he has looked after himself, and banished from myself avarice, desire, and anger, as he has banished them from himself, as great courage would be perceptible in me as we perceive in him.—ANOTHER said: Until this day I used to dread the approach of death; now what I fear is the protraction of life.—ZENO: You are better able to attain death than to protract life.—He answered: My weariness of life does not induce me to summon death myself, before it comes to me.—ZENO: We have known friends do much to see the friend who has not seen them; if you love death, what prevents your seeking it before it seek you?—He answered: Death is not a friend, but a bridge which men must pass before they can arrive at that which they desire and love.—ZENO: Then why do you remain, although you know for certain that death will make you nobler?—He answered: I am like a guardian of the frontier-pass who, if he abide, abides with regret, and if he advance and conquer, will attain to honour.—ZENO: What is the meaning of your parable?—He said: The soul of the philosopher is stationed at the pass, its pass being the body; on the other side are wants, lusts, and passions. Every soul has sore trouble in dealing with these enemies, and in keeping them away. The glory consists in the joy and pleasure whereto the soul attains at parting.—When their discussion had reached this point, another named STEPHANUS(?) said: If the name of 'philosopher' have no other use than to preserve its owner from the name of 'ignorant,' why should I make any effort to obtain it?—Another said: Merely for the sake of honour I would not seek this name.—ZENO said: Did I desire this name for nothing else, I should desire it for the sake of obtaining security from the fear and horror of death.—KRITON said: The greatest of the benefits of that science is that it makes for us many cares into one.—KRAMAS(?) said: Since in this world one thing alone, sorrow, is permanent, the most profitable thing for us to sympathize with is the high aim of one who is concerned about a thing that is everlasting.—PINDAR said: All men are at war, and the fittest enemy for the warrior to attack is the enemy nearest home; and that enemy is the trouble of his own breast.— ELETUS (Theaetetus?) said: Who are the philosopher's enemies?—PIN-DAR said: His most particular enemies are the pleasures of his breast, which hinder his search after wisdom.—When the discourse of these people had reached this point, SIMMIAS, turning to Aristotle, said: Enlighten our hearts with the rays of thy lamp ere its light be quenched, good father!—ARISTOTLE: The most acquisitive of scholars is he who acquires no knowledge until he has disciplined himself and corrected himself; the most accurate of speakers is he who attempts not to speak save after meditation, and the soundest of workers is he who acts only after deliberation. And no one more needs deliberation and caution in carrying out a plan, than the philosopher in undertaking matters of which the trouble is present and the reward prospective. First let him meditate; then, when meditation brings sight, let him make sight his guide to action; and if sight show that the action will be remunerative, then let him endure the trouble of doing before he reaps the fruit. And when after seeing he resolves to undertake the work, at the time when he should reap the fruit he ought not to be vexed at the trouble he has endured. For he who weans his soul from pleasures and undertakes the labour of searching for wisdom for the sake of God, and to gain the reward therefor after death, if at the hour of death he exhibits melancholy, makes himself an object of laughter and derision. So too does he become an object of laughter and derision who makes a feast and lays the foundation of a palace, and when about to attain the purpose of his feast and of the building of his palace becomes sad and gloomy. I have known men who have undertaken this task while in doubt concerning the reward—nor is there any wonder that one who is in doubt concerning the recompense after death should be grieved and sorrowful about dying—but I do wonder at any one who is grieved at death while professing to believe in a recompense after death.—When Aristotle had brought this discourse to a conclusion, KRITON said: If you desire us to be contented after your departure, O worthy teacher! the eloquent speech which you have made must increase our sorrow at your departure; and if death be profitable to you, to us it is most detrimental, on account of the unsolved difficulties remaining among us for which you were our refuge.—DIOGENES said: The same thing cannot be profitable to one thing and detrimental to another unless there be some contrariety between the two latter; if Aristotle's departure be profitable to himself and detrimental to us, this must be because of some difference between us.—KRITON: There is both agreement and diversity between us and him; we agree in our wish and desire, and differ about our remaining and his departure—DIOGENES: Your grief comes not of his being about to enter the house of honour, but rather of your remaining in the abode of disgrace.—LYSIAS said: You both speak well. You were the pillars of a hall wherein were lamps; the greatest pillar has fallen, and the weight has come upon the other pillars; the most brilliant lamp is extinguished, the light in the hall is diminished, and the darkness increased. Nor is it the falling of the pillar nor the extinction of the lamp that troubles you; but rather the darkness of the hall and the weight of the roof.—SIMMIAS, glancing at Aristotle, said: O guide to wisdom! tell us what is the first thing which it behoves the seeker after wisdom to acquire? —ARISTOTLE: Seeing that the soul is the source of wisdom, the first knowledge which is profitable for him is knowledge of the soul—SIM-

MIAS: How should he seek it?—ARISTOTLE: By his own virtue.—SIM-MIAS: What is his own virtue?—ARISTOTLE: That virtue whereby you asked me about yourself.—SIMMIAS: How is it possible for any one to ask any one else about himself?—ARISTOTLE: Even as the sick man asks the physician about himself, and even as the blind man might ask those about him of his own colour.—SIMMIAS: How can the self be blind about the self, when the self is the source of all sight?—ARIS-TOTLE: When wisdom is secreted and concealed in the self, that is the soul, it is blind to itself, and to others alike: even as the eye without the light of a lamp is blind both to itself and others.—SIMMIAS: Then the learner can only learn through wisdom, and the seer can only see with a lamp.—ARISTOTLE: The soul becomes capable of receiving wisdom only by its natural correctness, and the sight of the seer becomes penetrating only through a lamp. When the two come together, it can penetrate.—SIMMIAS: If the soul and the eyes cannot attain brightness in their functions by their own virtue, unaided by wisdom and the lamplight, then nothing is nearer akin to the soul than wisdom.—ARIS-TOTLE: How can anything be nearer akin to that which it takes in than its own source? Do you not see that the teacher has a better right to the name of knowledge than the taught? and that the possessor of force has a better title to the name of force than one who is ac-quiring it? For the teacher is the source of knowledge, seeing that knowledge flows from him, and the strong is the source of strength.—When the discourse reached this point, LYSIAS said: This subject is finished, and I will now begin afresh. Tell me how it is that knowledge of the soul is the worthiest thing for the acquirer to acquire first?—ARISTOTLE: Because knowledge is an essential property of teacher and taught.—LYSIAS: How am I to know that knowledge is a property of the soul?—ARISTOTLE said: Because knowledge is in the body only so long as the soul is in it; and when the soul is separated from the body, knowledge disappears from it.—LYSIAS: It may come from the body rather than the soul.—ARISTOTLE: If it were of the body, it would ap-pear in the dead body as much as in the living body.—LYSIAS: We are as ignorant of the knowledge of the dead, as we are of their ignorance. May it be that the *ignorance* of it which we do not know may come from the fact that the soul is departed from it?—ARISTOTLE: If ignor-ance be blindness to one's own concerns, then the ignorance and blindness of the body before death are even more evident than its ignorance after death.—LYSIAS: Though the ignorance of blindness may be in the body after death, the ignorance of folly is not there assuredly.—ARISTOTLE: What is the difference between the ignorance of blindness and the ignorance of folly?—LYSIAS: Wherein is the iden-tity?—ARISTOTLE: The two are identical in that they both afflict people

[65]

of understanding. As for the ignorance of folly, it is like badness and evil-doing and evil-speaking; and as for the ignorance of blindness, it is like an evil smell and the fetid matter whence it proceeds.—LYSIAS: I only know of the existence of foulness and sensuality while the soul is in the body: can it be that this foulness proceeds from the soul and not from the body?—ARISTOTLE: If foul habits were of the original essence of the soul, while the soul was abstracted from accidental states, this foulness would appear in every soul, and no soul would be without it; how then could we have learned that the philosopher's soul is free from foulness, and uncleanness? Whereas we have learned and know well that the purity of their souls has gained the upper hand over lust and overcome desire and passion. They have subdued these inclinations and harmonized lust with reason.—LYSIAS: If then between lust and the soul there be so great a difference, how comes it that passion and the soul part together from the body?—ARISTOTLE: The soul is a flame, and when some one of the humours of the body prevails, it kindles the body as fire kindles fuel, and causes the light of the soul to issue from the body even as a fire brings brightness and heat out of wood. And passion is as a fire that brings the brightness of the soul out of the body.—LYSIAS: Can it be that brightness itself comes from warmth?—ARISTOTLE: If brightness varied with heat, a summer night should be brighter than a winter day, even as a summer night is warmer than a winter day.—When the dialogue had reached this point, LYSIAS said: You have enlivened my mind, O teacher! this discourse is worthy of deep consideration. Most assuredly I must endeavour to distinguish between soul and passion, the heat of the latter and the brightness of the former. You have made clear to me each of the two, passion and the body, and the distinction of the soul from both, according to their attributes. Now, I would have you show the distinction between the conduct of the soul and of the passion, even as you have shown the distinction between themselves.—ARISTOTLE: Do you know of any distinction between their functions?—LYSIAS: I know not of any distinction between their substance, but only between their functions: but I would fain have you show me the difference between the conduct of the one and that of the other by signs clear enough to distinguish the work of the one from that of the other.—ARISTOTLE: All that is bad is the work of the passion and all that is good is the work of the soul.—LYSIAS: I know the difference between the good conduct of the one and the foul action of the other no better than the difference between their substances.—ARISTOTLE: Good action or goodness is that which, when it comes to you, puts you right; and badness is that which, when it comes to you, does you harm.—LYSIAS: Nothing has ever come to me which has done good to a part of me but has damaged some other part. How can I call it "good" when I never have found it free from harm?—ARISTOTLE: When the thing that is beneficial benefits that part of you which you are more bound to love than to hate, be not vexed if it harm some part of you which you are more bound to hate than to love.—LYSIAS: What part of me is it which I am bound to hate, and what, that I am bound to love?—ARISTOTLE: You should love your intellect and hate your unintelligent part.—LYSIAS: What comes of this?—ARISTOTLE: Why, nothing increases your intellect but that which lessens your non-intelligence. Love therefore that which improves your intellect, even though it lessen your non-intelligence. For the advantage done you by it in decreasing your non-intelligence is not inferior to that done you by the improvement of your intellect.—LYSIAS: You distinguished between soul and passion by your illustration of heat and light; and you showed me the difference of their functions by showing the difference of their origin. I then asked you to make clear to me what they each do by some sign which should sever the work of the one from the work of the other; you then told me that well-doing was the work of the soul and ill-doing the work of the passion. I asked you the difference between good and bad actions. You answered that whatever increases the intellect is a good action even though non-intelligence is increased by it, and whatever causes decrease of intellect is bad, even though it increase the non-intelligence. Neither intelligence nor non-intelligence is diminished except by its opposite, nor increased except by what agrees with it. Now, I still require an explanation of what it is that increases the intelligence and what it is that lessens it.—ARISTOTLE said: Whatsoever adds brightness to your vision of things increases your intelligence, and whatsoever makes things dark to you lessens it.—LYSIAS said: What is it that gives them brightness, and what is it that veils them?—ARISTOTLE: Truth-speaking and whatever resembles it is an illuminator, doubt and whatever resembles it a cloke.—LYSIAS said: I understand how true-speaking illuminates and how doubt darkens; but what are the things *which resemble them?*—ARISTOTLE: Right-doing or justice resembles true-speaking, and injustice or iniquity resembles falsehood and doubt.—LYSIAS: In what respect do justice and veracity resemble each other?—ARISTOTLE: Each of them consists in leaving things in their own places.—LYSIAS: And in what respect do falsehood and injustice resemble each other?—ARISTOTLE: Each consists in removing things from their own places.—LYSIAS: Justice and injustice are the work of administrators and judges only; whereas I am asking you concerning things in general—ARISTOTLE: All men are judges, only some private, others public. He whose judgment errs, and whose tongue speaks false, and whosoever appropriates what is not his, such a man is unjust and a liar: whereas he who sees things aright, and whose tongue speaks the truth, and who is satisfied with what is his, is righteous, just, and veracious. Nor is any human action outside the two patterns which we have described.—LYSIAS: How am I to know that nothing falls out of these two kinds?—ARISTOTLE: Enquire among the events which are passing and have passed over you, whether any of them lies outside these patterns. If none such be found, include those events which have not yet passed over you among those which have passed over you.—LYSIAS: How am I to include what has not yet happened to me with what has happened, and pass the same judgment upon it? —ARISTOTLE: If the few be part of the many things, and the parts of a thing resemble the whole, then the few things which you see belong to the many things which you do not see, and it is probable that the many things which you do not see are like what you do see. If this reasoning be correct, then you may well pass the same judgment upon the good and evil which have not yet happened to you as upon the good and evil which have happened to you.—LYSIAS: What should make me judge of the absent as of the present?—ARISTOTLE: That which is present must necessarily make you pass a judgment on what is absent; or the thing which makes you know the absence of the absent from knowing the presence of the present.—LYSIAS: What prevents my knowing the present without knowing the absent? Or how is my knowledge of the absent increased by my knowledge of the present? That portion of the earth which I see does not show me the portion which is beyond; neither does my not seeing the portion to which my eye cannot reach hinder my seeing the portion which I can see.—ARISTOTLE: But do not you pass judgment that beyond the earth which we see there is the earth which we do not see? Similarly must you not necessarily pass judgment that beyond those events which have happened to you are those which have not happened, even as you passed judgment that beyond the portion of the earth which you saw there was the earth which you did not see?—LYSIAS: I am constrained to admit that I must judge by the absent of the present. Only tell me this: If I pass no judgment from the present on the absent, does my knowledge of the present suffer any detriment? By knowing which I may derive benefit in judging of the absent from the present.—ARISTOTLE: No one knows a thing who is unable to distinguish it from what differs from it.—LYSIAS: How so?—ARISTOTLE: If the saying of the wise DARIUS be true, that no one knows the truth who cannot discriminate it from the false, and no one knows what is right who cannot sever it from what is wrong, then so long as you are not acquainted with the absent, you have no means of knowing the present.—LYSIAS: This subject is over. Now, O guide to philosophy! I would ask you this: Is it possible to embrace in one notion all those things concerning the baseness of which mankind are agreed, fornication, theft, drunkenness, deceit, injustice, treachery, fraud, malice, envy, ignorance, pride, self-complacency, so as to exclude nothing, whereby I might know that the events which have not yet passed over me are like to those which have passed over me?—ARISTOTLE: The possessors of these qualities and characteristics are unjust, false, and self-blinding, insomuch as they strive after what is not theirs.—LYSIAS: How so?—ARISTOTLE: Do you not see that no one sets about any of these iniquities before avarice, desire, or anger bestir itself in him, after which he sets about them. Now with avarice, desire, and passion reason cannot remain at peace. And the reason being out of order, it cannot take the right path, and whoso does not take the right path goes astray; he that goes astray is a wrong-doer, and the wrong-doer and the liar are in torment.—LYSIAS: You have collected under one notion all the vices; could you do the same for the virtues?—ARISTOTLE: To abandon injustice is to adhere to justice and right; and to avoid the false is to strain after the true. If the foulness of the vices has been made clear to you, it must inevitably have been made clear that virtue consists in abandoning vice.—LYSIAS: Is there any mean between vice and virtue? so that having got rid of vice I might not attain to virtue, but remain at the mean; like one who, abandoning falsehood, stops short at silence and speaks neither truth nor falsehood; or one who avoids iniquity and does neither injustice nor justice?—ARISTOTLE: He who is silent elects to be so either with ignorance or with knowledge; if he be silent with knowledge, he is a speaker of truth; if with ignorance he is a liar. So, too, whoso pauses does so either for fraud or for right; if for right, he is just and righteous; if for fraud, he is iniquitous and a doer of injustice.—LYSIAS: You have made clear to me the difference between all the good and the bad that may happen to me by a clear distinction, and have proved to me that whatever has not happened to me must resemble what has happened. God, who gave thee wisdom, and who protects thee, give thee therefor a meet reward! Never has father in his lifetime tended his child better, or after death left him a more honourable inheritance!—ARISTOTLE: If you are satisfied with the answer to your questions, let Kriton speak, for I can see that he wishes to do so.—KRITON: It is painful to impose on you the burden of speaking, whereas it is sad to be quiet and leave the subject to be finished on some later day.—ARISTOTLE: Withhold nothing, so long as you see a spark of life in me on which I can sustain myself.—KRITON: I heard and understood all the answers you gave Lysias; and I agreed as he did that the absent is to be known from the present. But I am not quite satisfied without knowing what are the qualities and unknown operations of that "absent" to which I confessed and agreed.—ARISTOTLE: I know of nothing in the present or the absent, save knowledge and ignorance, and the reward of the two.—KRITON: How could I acknowledge this of the "absent and the present," when I have not yet acknowledged it of the present? And though you should force me to acknowledge it of the present, I will not acknowledge it of the absent, save by definition and evidence.—ARISTOTLE: The evidence which tells you it of the present will also tell it of the absent.—KRITON: What evidence?—ARISTOTLE: Do you not agree that the right way in seeking the truth is what SOKRATES said?—KRITON: And what did he say?— ARISTOTLE: I am told that he said, Whenever you are in difficulty about a question, give it two alternatives, one of which must necessarily be true; then proceed till one of the two is refuted, for with the refutation of the one alternative will come the establishment of the other.—KRITON: Yes, I have observed that he acted thus in difficult investigations. Now what evidence have you about the nature of the present and absent?—ARISTOTLE: Do you not grant that there is nothing outside knowledge and its contrary?—KRITON: I must do so.—ARISTOTLE: Do you grant that things are bettered only by their like, and damaged only by what is unlike them?—KRITON: Undoubtedly.—ARISTOTLE: Then do you not see that if the recompense of knowledge be not like it, it must be the contrary of it? And, if it be the contrary of knowledge, then the recompense of the wise will be ignorance, and the recompense of the seeing blindness, and the recompense of well-doing ill-doing? Now such as this would not be a *recompense* but a *punishment.* Then whoever bears the burden of knowledge must allow that he will gain no recompense for it. This judgment being false, the opposite of it is true. The recompense for seeing will be sight; for well-doing, good; for seeking wisdom, finding wisdom.—KRITON: You have forced me to agree that knowledge will be rewarded and ignorance punished.—ARISTOTLE: If you are satisfied that the recompense of the ignorant is the reverse of the recompense of the wise—otherwise the reward of blindness would be sight and that of goodness badness, and that of hating wisdom obtaining wisdom. Now such a view or doctrine must be false in the eyes of him who has borne the labour of pursuing knowledge in the hope of the reward thereof, and in order to avoid the penalty of ignorance. This opinion being proved false makes the opposite necessarily true.—KRITON: This argument applies as forcibly to me, since I have borne the burden of the searcher after knowledge with a view to the reward thereof, and have avoided ignorance fearing its penalty. But what will you say if I withdraw this concession, and deny that knowledge is rewarded and ignorance punished?—ARISTOTLE: Then what induces you to discuss and to argue with me? The desire for the benefit of knowledge and the endeavour to avoid the harm of ignorance or something else?—KRITON: Nay, desire for the benefit of knowledge and the endeavour to avoid the harm of ignorance induce me to do this.—ARISTOTLE: Then you have acknowledged that knowledge is beneficial and ignorance detrimental. Now a reward is not other than beneficial, and a penalty is not other than detrimental. —KRITON: I acknowledge that wisdom is beneficial during life, not after death.—ARISTOTLE: What is the advantage of knowledge during life? A pleasant life or increase of knowledge?—KRITON: I granted the value of knowledge, and I have seen that knowledge is detrimental to the pleasures of life; it necessarily follows that the advantage of knowledge must be in the next world.—ARISTOTLE: If you doubt the benefits accruing to the wise in the next world, while knowledge precludes the enjoyment of this world, it is impossible for you to assert that knowledge is of value in either world.—KRITON: I see that if I grant that knowledge is beneficial, I must acknowledge that it is so in the next world. I will now deny that it possesses any advantage, in order to be able to deny that it is of advantage in the next world.— ARISTOTLE: Do you not then prefer hearing, seeing, and understanding to blindness, deafness, and folly?—KRITON: Yes.—ARISTOTLE: Do you prefer them for the sake of some advantage or not?—KRITON: For the sake of some advantage.—ARISTOTLE: Once again then you have acknowledged that there is some advantage; and you have the same conclusion forced on you as before.—KRITON: I have ever acknowledged the value of knowledge, so long as I live, in respect of the comfort and peace that I gain from it, and the pain of ignorance that I am freed from; but I know of no other benefit therefrom.—ARISTOTLE: Then is there anything else beyond this which is otherwise than it?—KRITON: What evidence is there that there is anything else beyond this, which exists after death and is as it was in life?—ARISTOTLE: Now death is nothing else but the soul surviving the body?—KRITON: It is nothing else.—ARISTOTLE: Then is anything "absent" which is benefited in absence except by that whereby it is also benefited in presence?—KRITON: It must be so.—ARISTOTLE: Then why do you ask what it is from which the soul derives benefit in the state of absence from the body other than that from which it derives benefit in the state of presence? Or, what can harm it in the state of absence that does not harm it likewise in the state of presence?—KRITON: You have left me no loophole to deny the value of knowledge in this world and the next, and the harm of ignorance in both; these I must acknowledge, and I allow that you are right in stating that in the present and the absent I know of nothing save knowledge, ignorance, and the recompense of the two. It may be, however, there is something besides these which others

[71]

have learned, though I have not.—ARISTOTLE: Can an answer be given but after a question?—KRITON: No.—ARISTOTLE: Can a question ever be asked before that which is asked about comes into the mind?—KRITON: No.—ARISTOTLE: If you have a clear notion of that about which you have asked, you have obtained the answer thereto in the answer which you received to your question about knowledge, ignorance, and their recompense. But if you have no notion in your own mind of that about which you would ask, I am not bound to reply.—KRITON: True, my question was not justified, and no answer is due from you. I have obtained the answer to my question.—ARISTOTLE: Then give Simmias leave to speak in his turn.—SIMMIAS said: I heard all that Lysias asked concerning your statements, and the replies you gave Kriton: and all is clear to me except one word that Kriton accepted from you, but which is not clear to me as yet.—ARISTOTLE: Which?—SIMMIAS: I heard you say that there is nothing either in "absence" or "presence" except knowledge, its opposite, and the recompense of the two. Now how can it be clear to me that there is nothing save this?—ARISTOTLE: Do you know of anything else?—SIMMIAS: I know of the heavens and the earth, the mountains and the plains, the animals, and all else that is on the dry and the moist, which I cannot call knowledge, nor ignorance, nor the recompense of either without proof.—ARISTOTLE: Do you agree with the saying of HERMES, quoted by me in the book of physics?—SIMMIAS: What is that saying?—ARISTOTLE: HERMES states that no object acquires strength except by union with its like; and that none acquires weakness except by union with what is unlike it.—SIMMIAS: Yes, it is so; there is nothing in which experience does not show the truth of Hermes' saying.—ARISTOTLE: Then you have acknowledged that nothing exists except knowledge, ignorance, and the recompense of the two.—SIMMIAS: How so?—ARISTOTLE: Of the things which you have enumerated there is none that does not belong to this world.—SIMMIAS: Certainly.—ARISTOTLE: Know you what it is that induces philosophers to abandon this world?—SIMMIAS: Their knowledge, by seeing that these things are detrimental to the intellect, induces them to take this course. —ARISTOTLE: Then have you not learned that whatever harms the intellect is the opposite of the intellect, and the opposite of the intellect is non-intelligence?—SIMMIAS: If what you say, that these things harm the intellect, be true of the earth, it is not true of the heaven.—ARISTOTLE: Nay, the heaven differs not from the earth in this matter.—SIMMIAS: In what respect are the heavens as detrimental to the intellect as the earth?—ARISTOTLE: The least detriment occasioned to knowledge by the heaven is this, that it prevents the sight from penetrating and passing through; now that which is inimical to sight is inimical to intelligence.—SIMMIAS: This theory is true of the present; what of the absent?—ARISTOTLE: The absent must either be like or unlike the present, must it not?—SIMMIAS: Yes.—ARISTOTLE: If it be like it, must it not help its like? If it be unlike, must it not oppose it and thwart it? —SIMMIAS: Now, indeed, I must certainly agree to all that Kriton accepted from you. Now tell me the explanation of a single saying that I have met with in the works of the great PLATO: that everything that does good averts ill; but not everything that averts ill does good; and that the philosopher should amass a great quantity of those things which both avert ill and do good, and be content with a small number of those things which avert ill but do no good.—ARISTOTLE: Plato tells you that only those things suit the philosopher which bring him good and avert ill from him; and thereby he means knowledge which brings illumination to the mind and averts the darkness of ignorance; and he bids him acquire much of it. And of that which averts ill but is unprofitable, which is food, clothing and lodging, he bids him be content with as much as is absolutely necessary, because to exceed the limit in these things does harm to the intellect, whereas to seek the mean averts ill, but does no positive good, since none of the pleasures of knowledge proceeds therefrom to the mind. Hence it behoves the philosopher to be easily satisfied with obtaining the means of subsistence and very eager to acquire knowledge.—SIMMIAS: What is it that prevents that which averts ill from doing positive good when both agree in averting ill?—ARISTOTLE: That which does positive good differs from that which averts ill in this, that whatever averts ill only, if it be pursued to excess, ceases even to avert ill, and becomes detrimental; whereas that which does positive good, *i.e.* knowledge, the more there is of it the more beneficial it is; whereas that which averts ill only does so, so long as it in moderation. Do you not see that if you are satisfied with a modicum of food, it averts the mischief of hunger? similarly drink and clothing; whereas all, if there be more of them than is necessary, become detrimental, and their power of averting ill even is annulled, like heavy armour which wounds or kills its bearer. Whereas that which both does good and averts ill (that is, wisdom), however much there be of it, does not, like heavy armour, weigh down its possessor. Thus did Plato distinguish between that which does good and that which averts ill, according to what you heard of his sayings.—SIMMIAS: Is there any other term besides these two or not? —ARISTOTLE: One other term remains; if it be added to these others, nothing is left out.—SIMMIAS: What is that?—ARISTOTLE: Things are of three sorts: the thing which both does good and averts ill; that which averts ill, but induces no good; and that which does harm.—SIMMIAS: What is it that does harm?—ARISTOTLE: A thing which averts ill, when carried to excess, so as to become detrimental.—SIMMIAS: This subject is concluded. My mind is as much brightened by your instruction as the eye of the seer by the light of day. Now tell me: Is there any affinity between that which gives brightness to the mind and that which gives brightness to the eye? Or, is there any resemblance between the mind and the eye?—ARISTOTLE: They are things which do not resemble each other so much in substance as in function. If you have received the answer to your question, let Diogenes speak.—Simmias became silent.—DIOGENES then said: I have observed that those philosophers whose mental vision has been most acute have been the most temperate. Now tell me: Do goodness and temperance spring from brightness of mental vision or not?—ARISTOTLE: There are different sorts of passions and divers sorts of intellects. Over against each passion there is an intellect best capable of opposing that passion. Lust in its nature is not the essence of folly, but each is a separate essence, though both are at one in harming the philosopher and keeping him from his recompense. Nor again is that faculty and quality which recommends self-restraint identical with the faculty and quality which overcomes folly and brings knowledge; neither are they opposed to each other; rather is there resemblance and also diversity between the two, like the resemblance and diversity between running water and ice; the one being fine and rare, the other hard and coarse; just so is fine ignorance opposed to fine knowledge, and strong piety to strong lust. And if a man's habit of temperance is weak and his property of knowledge strong, his judgment sees aright, while his conduct, so far as continence goes, is weak; while the intellectual vision and the conduct of him whose case is the opposite are opposite.—DIOGENES: How can this be right, when you have said before that nothing exists except knowledge, ignorance, and the recompense of each? *Now* you have acknowledged the existence of knowledge, ignorance, continence, lust, and other things.—ARISTOTLE: Do you not see that running water and ice resemble each other? Similar to this is the resemblance of lust to ignorance, and the rest are like this too. Being similar in operation they become one in name.—DIOGENES: How do I know that ignorance is to lust as running water to ice?—ARISTOTLE: Do you not see that both hurt the intellect, just as running water and ice neither tolerate heat?—DIOGENES: This subject is over. Now tell me: Which science is the most proper for me to pursue?—ARISTOTLE: Since the pursuit of philosophy is the best of the pursuits of this world, and the recompense therefor is the greatest of the recompense of the next world, philosophy is the best science that you can pursue.—DIOGENES: Is there any other knowledge besides philosophy or not?—ARISTOTLE: The vulgar herd have a sort of knowledge and science and truth and honesty and generosity and other wasted virtues, which are as different from wisdom

as the form of an animal is from a picture or sketch on a wall.—Diogenes: Why do you call those virtues of the vulgar herd *wasted*?—
Aristotle: On account of the ignorance of the vulgar with regard to
them.—Diogenes: How so?—Aristotle: Because the vulgar wise man
brings his knowledge into play there where it will not increase his
gain, and their merciful man spares him who is worthy of exemplary
punishment, and their veracious man brings his veracity into play
when it pleases him, though the truth be obscene, and their liberal
man is liberal to the unworthy, and their faithful man keeps his
promises to people's ruin, and their hearer hears to no purpose. Beyond
a doubt these good qualities are wasted in them, and no more resemble
the virtues of the wise than a painting on a wall resembles a living
animal.—Diogenes: How does your illustration correspond with the
virtues of the few and of the many?—Aristotle: Have you not learned
that knowledge is life and ignorance death?—Diogenes: Yes.—Aristotle: The knowledge of the wise man vivifies his actions, whereas
the folly of the ignorant mortifies his.—Diogenes: Then are their good
actions any better than their bad ones or not?—Aristotle: They are
not.—Diogenes: How so?—Aristotle: The well-doer of the vulgar
intends to do good, and takes a wrong path. The evil-doer among them
intends evil and carries it out in the wrong way. They are just alike
and neither has the advantage.—Diogenes: I know now in what way
their virtues are wasted. Now show the superiority of wisdom without
which no actions are profitable.—Aristotle: Whosoever has seen good,
abandoned evil, and entered into goodness has acted in accordance
with wisdom; and whosoever has intended good and erred, or intended
evil and carried it out, has departed from wisdom.—Diogenes: This
whole subject is clear. Now tell me: To whom was this thing, I mean
wisdom, first made clear?—Aristotle: The minds of men are far from
being able to attain to any thing so grand without teaching; just as
their eyes are far from seeing without the light of a lamp.—Diogenes:
From whom did the philosophers learn it?—Aristotle: The heralds
and ambassadors of the different ages in the different regions of the
globe were constantly summoning mankind thereunto; and the first
person on earth to whom that knowledge came by revelation was
Hermes.—Diogenes: Whence came it to Hermes?—Aristotle: His
mind was taken up to heaven and it came to him from the Archangels,
who had got it from the record of God. From him it came to the
earth, and was received by the sages.—Diogenes: How am I to know
that Hermes obtained that knowledge from the inhabitants of heaven?
—Aristotle: If that knowledge be the truth, it can come from above.
—Diogenes: Why?—Aristotle: Do you not see that the upper part of
each thing is better than the lower? The upper part of water and its

surface are purer than the lower; the higher parts of the earth are pleasanter and fairer than the lower parts; the best member of a man is his head, the purest thing in a tree is its fruit; and so on with everything. The fittest thing, therefore, to come from on high is wisdom. Another proof is this: the substance and nature of wisdom have overcome and outtopped everything else.—DIOGENES: O guide to wisdom! Our minds vary not the least from thine. Make a compact between us which will guard us from differing with one another!—ARISTOTLE: If you would follow my ways, imitate my books.—DIOGENES: There are so many. Which will settle differences between us best if any such arise?—ARISTOTLE: Questions concerning the "first science" and the science of theology you should seek from the book of Hermes; for difficulties in the way of politics [you should go to the Politics, and for] difficulties in natural science, to the Physics; for difficulties about good and bad actions, to the Ethics; whereas if any difference arise among you about the definitions of speech, you should refer to the four books of Logic, the first *the Categories,* the second περὶ ἑρμηνείας, the third ἀναλυτική, the fourth ἀποδεικτική, or book of Demonstration, which tells you how to distinguish between true and false. There you will obtain light on dark matters.

When Aristotle had spoken thus far, his soul became powerless; his hand shook, and the apple fell out of his hand. The philosophers all rose and came near to him, and kissed his hand and eyes and eulogized him. He grasped KRITON's hand and laid it on his face saying, "I commit my spirit to the Receiver of the spirits of the wise." Then he ceased and his spirit passed away. His friends lamented over him, saying, "The day of knowledge is over."

Bibliography

I. Texts of the Latin version of The Apple

Plezia, Marianus. *Aristotelis qui ferebatur Liber de Pomo. Auctorum Graecorum et Latinorum Opuscula. Selecta II.* Varsoviae: Academia Scientiarum Polona, 1960.

Plezia, Marianus. "Aristotelis qui ferebatur liber *De Pomo.* Versio latina vetusta interprete Manfredo duce." *Eos,* 47 (1954), pp. 191-217.

II. English translations of The Apple

Gollancz, Hermann. *The Targum to "The Song of Songs"; The Book of the Apple; The Ten Jewish Martyrs; A Dialogue on Games of Chance. Translated from the Hebrew and Aramaic.* London: Luzac and Co., 1908.

Kalisch, Isidor. *Ha-Tapuach: The Apple. A Treatise on the Immortality of the Soul by Aristotle the Stagyrite. Translated from the Hebrew with Notes and Aphorisms.* New York: The American Hebrew. 1885.

Margoliouth, D. S. "*The Book of the Apple* ascribed to Aristotle edited in Persian and English." *The Journal of the Royal Asiatic Society of Great Britain and Ireland,* n.s. XXIV (1892), pp. 187-252.

III. Works about The Apple

Hertz, Wilhelm. "Das Buch vom Apfel," in Friedrich von der Leyen (ed.) *Gesammelte Abhandlungen von Wilhelm Hertz.* Stuttgart und Berlin: J. G. Cotta'sche Buchhandlung Nachfolger. 1905.

Kraemer, Jörg. "Das Arabische Original des pseudo-aristotelischen Liber de Pomo." In *Studi Orientalistici in onore di G. Levi della Vida.* Rome. 1956.

Plezia, Marianus. "Neues zum pseudoaristotelischen Buch vom Apfel," *Philologisches Vorträge,* 1959, pp. 191-96.

Plezia, Marianus. *Ps. Arystotelesowy Traktat De Pomo. Sprawozdania . . . Polskiej Akademii Umiejetnosci* LIII, 1952.

IV. Catalogues of Manuscripts

Ethé, H. *Persian Manuscripts of the Bodleian Library.* n.p., 1889.

Gesamtkatalog Der Wiegendrucke. Leipzig: Karl W. Hiersemann, 1926.

Lacombe, Georgius, A. Birkenmajer, M. Dulong et Aet. Franceschini. *Aristoteles Latinus, Pars Prior.* Paris: Desclée de Brouwer, 1939, reprinted 1957. *Pars Posterior,* Cantabrigiae: Typis Academiae, 1955. *Supplementa Altera.* Paris: Desclée de Brouwer. 1961.

Steinschneider, Moritz. *Die Hebraeischen Übersetzungen des Mittelalters und die Juden als Dolmetscher.* Graz: Akademische Druck-U. Verlagsanstalt, 1956.

Stillwell, Margaret Bingham. *Incunabula and Americana 1450-1800,* New York: Columbia University Press. 1930.

V. Works on the history of philosophy
A. On Plato

Burnet, John. *Plato's Phaedo edited with Introduction and Notes.* Oxford: The Clarendon Press. 1911.

Hackforth, R. *Plato's Phaedo Translated with Introduction and Commentary.* Cambridge: University Press. 1955.

Klibansky, Raymond. *The Continuity of the Platonic Tradition.* London: The Warburg Institute. 1939.

Walzer, R. "Aflatun." *Encyclopedia of Islam.* Ed. H. A. R. Gibb *et al.* London: Luzac and Co., 1960. col. I, pp. 230-235.

Walzer, Richard. *Galeni Compendium Timaei Platonis. Plato Arabus.* vol. I. London: Warburg Institute. 1951.

[77]

B. On Aristotle

Abel, Armand. *Aristote, La légende et l'histoire*. Bruxelles: Office de Publicité. 1944.

Bardenhewer, Otto. *Die pseudo-aristotelische Schrift Ueber das reine Gute bekannt unter dem Namen Liber de Causis*. Freiburg im Breisgau. Herder'sche Verlagshandlung. 1882.

Birkenmajer, Alexandre. *Classement des ouvrages attribués à Aristote par le moyen âge Latin*. Cracovie: Imprimerie de l'Université de Cracovie. 1932.

Chroust, Anton-Hermann. "A Contribution to the Medieval Discussion: Utrum Aristoteles Sit Salvatus." *Journal of the History of Ideas*, 6 (1945), pp. 231-38.

Düring, Ingemar. *Aristotle in the Ancient Biographical Tradition*. Goteborg: Elanders Boktryckeri Aktiebolag. 1957.

Ginzberg, Louis. "Aristotle in Jewish Legend." *The Jewish Encyclopedia*. New York: Ktav Publishing House, Inc. 1901. Vol. II, pp. 98-99.

Grabmann, Martin. *Forschungen uber die Latienischen Aristoteles-übersetzungen des XIII. Jh.* Beiträge zur Geschichte der Philosophie des Mittelalters XVII, 5-6. Münster. 1916.

Grabmann, Martin. *I divieti ecclesiastici di Aristotele sotto Innocenzo III e Gregorio IX*. Romae: Typis Pontificiae Universitatis Gregorianae. 1941.

Rees, D. A. "Theories of the Soul in the Early Aristotle." In Düring, I. and G. E. L. Owen, *Aristotle and Plato in the Mid-Fourth Century*. Goteborg: n.p. 1960.

Thorndike, Lynn. "The Latin Pseudo-Aristotle and Medieval Occult Science," *Journal of English and Germanic Philology*. XXI (1922), pp. 229-58.

Wingate, S. D. *The Medieval Latin Versions of the Aristotelian Scientific Corpus, with Special Reference to the Biological Works*. London: The Courier Press. 1931.

C. On other aspects of Greek thought

Henry, Paul and Hans-Rudolph Schwyzer (eds.). *Plotini Opera. Mvsevm Lessianvm Series Philosophica XXXIV*. Paris: Desclée de Brouwer et Cie. 1959.

MacKenna, Stephen (trans.). *Plotinus, The Enneads*. London: Faber and Faber, Ltd. 1956.

O'Leary, De Lacy. *How Greek Science Passed to the Arabs*. London: Routledge and Kegan Paul, Ltd. 1949.

Taylor, Thomas. *On Suicide*. London: n.p. 1834.

Wenrich, Johannes Georgius. *De Auctorum Graecorum Versionibus et Commentariis Syriacis Arabicis Armenicis Persicisque*. Lipsiae. 1842.

D. On Arabic and Persian thought

Bacher, S. W. *Nizami's Leben und Werke*. Leipzig. n.p. 1871.

Brockelmann, C. *Geschichte der Arabischen Litteratur. Erster Supplementband*. Leiden: E. J. Brill, 1937.

Clarke, H. Wilberforce (trans.). *The Sikander Nama, E Bara, or Book of Alexander the Great. Written A.D. 1200 by Abu Muhammed bin Yusuf bin Mu Ayyid-I-Nisami'd-Din*. London: W. H. Allen & Co. 1881.

Corbin, Henri. *Histoire de la philosophie islamique*. Paris: Gallimard, 1964.

Da Vaux, Carra. *Les penseurs de l'Islam*. Paris: Librarie Paul Geuthner, 1921-1926.

De Boer, T. J. *The History of Philosophy in Islam*. London: Luzac and Co. Ltd. 1961 reprint of 1903 edition.

Dieterici, F. H. *Die Philosophie der Araber im X. Jahrhundert n. Chr.* Leipzig: J. C. Hinrichs'sche Buchhandlung. 1876.

Flugel, G. *Al-Kindi gennant der Philosoph der Araber.* Leipzig: F. A. Brockhaus. 1857.

Leclerc, Lucien. *Histoire de la médicine arabe.* Paris: n.p. 1876.

Massignon, Louis. *Recueil de texts inédits concernant l'histoire de la mystique en pays d'Islam.* Paris: Librairie Orientaliste Paul Geuthner. 1929.

Mehren, A. F. "Correspondence du philosophe soufi ibn Sabin Abd Oul-Haqq avec l'Empéreur Frédéric II de Hohenstaufen." *Journal Asiatique,* vii série, tome xiv (Oct.-Dec. 1879), pp. 341-454.

Nicholson, Reynold A. *A Literary History of the Arabs.* Cambridge: The University Press. 1930.

Rescher, Nicholas. *Studies in Arabic Logic.* Pittsburgh: University of Pittsburgh Press. 1963.

Sachau, E. *Alberuni's India.* London: Kegan Paul, Ltd. 1910.

Sharif, M. M. (ed.). *A History of Muslim Philosophy.* Wiesbaden: Otto Harrassowitz. Vol. I, 1963. Vol. II, 1966.

Tibawi, A. L. "Ikhwan As-safa and their *Rasa'il,* A Critical Review of a Century and a Half of Research." *The Islamic Quarterly,* 2 (1955), pp. 28-45.

Walzer, Richard. "Arabic Transmission of Greek Thought to Medieval Europe." *Bulletin of the John Rylands Library.* No. 1, July, 1945. pp. 160-183.

Walzer, Richard. *Greek to Arabic. Essays on Islamic Philosophy.* Cambridge: Harvard University Press. 1962.

E. *On Hebrew thought*

Adler, H. (ed.). *Miscellany of Hebrew Literature.* London: N. Trubner and Co. 1872.

Dukes, Leopold. *Salomo ben Gabirol aus Malaga und die ethischen Werke desselben.* Hannover: Telgener'schen Hofbuchdruckerei. 1860.

Knowlton, Frank H. "Apple." *The Jewish Encyclopedia.* New York: Ktav Publishing House, Inc. 1901. Vol. II, pp. 23-24.

VI. *General Background Sources*

Allen, P. S. (ed.). *Opvs Epistolarvm Des. Erasmi Roterdami.* Oxonii: in Typographeo Clarendoniano. MCMXXXVIII.

Böhmer-Fischer. *Regesta imperii.* Innsbruck. n.p. 1879.

De Wulf, Maurice. *Histoire de la philosophie médiévale.* Louvain: Institut supérieur de philosophie. 1936.

de Ghellinck, J. *L'essor de la littérature latine au XII siècle.* Bruxelles-Bruges-Paris. 1955.

Deniflé, H. and E. Chatelain. *Chartularium Universitatis Parisiensis.* Paris. 1889.

Geyer, Bernhardus (ed.). *Alberti Magni Liber de Natura et Origine Animae.* Monasterii Westfalorum in Aedibus Aschendorff. 1955.

Geyer, Bernhard. *Die Patristische und Scholastische Philosophie.* Basel: Benno Schwabe und Co. 1951. Vol. II of Friedrich Ueberweg, *Grundriss der Geschichte der Philosophie.* Reprint of 1928 edition.

Gilson, Etienne. *History of Christian Philosophy in the Middle Ages.* New York: Random House. 1955.

Gordon, Peter. *L'image du monde dans l'antiquité.* Paris: Presses Universitaires de France. 1949.

Haskins, Charles Homer. *Studies in the History of Medieval Science.* Second edition. Cambridge: Harvard University Press. 1927.

Lecoy, F. "Sur la date du *Mors de la pomme.*" *Romania* LXXIV (1953), pp. 506 ff.

Lumby, Rev. Joseph Rawnon (ed.). *Polychronicon Ranulphi Higden Monachi Cestrensis, together with the English Translations of John Trevisa and of an Unknown Writer of the Fifteenth Century.* Vol. 41 of *Rerum Britannicarum Medii Aevi Scriptores, or the Chronicles and Memorials of Great Britain and Ireland during the Middle Ages.* London: Longman and Co. 1871.

[79]

Mandonnet, Pierre, O.P. *Siger de Brabant et l'Averroisme Latin au XIIIme siècle.*
  Louvain: Institut supérieur de philosophie de l'université. 1911.
Meerseman, P. G. *Opera Omnia B. Alberti Magni O.P.* Brugis: Carolum Beyaert.
  1931.
Salvatorelli, Luigi. *A Concise History of Italy.* New York: Oxford University
  Press. 1940.
Schirrmacher, F. *Die letzten Hohenstaufen.* Göttingen, n.p. 1871.
Thompson, Craig R. (trans.). *The Colloquies of Erasmus.* Chicago: The Univer-
  sity of Chicago Press. 1965.
Weinberg, Bernard. *A History of Literary Criticism in the Italian Renaissance.*
  Chicago: University of Chicago Press. 1961.

Mediaeval Philosophical Texts in Translation

Geoffrey of Vinsauf: Documentum De Modo Et Arte Dictandi Et Versificandi
trans. and intro. by Roger D. Parr, 116 pp., $3.00

St. Thomas, Siger de Brabant, St. Bonaventure: On the Eternity of the World
trans. by Cyril Vollert, S.J., Lottie Kendzierski, and Paul Byrne, 132 pp., $3.00

Francis Suarez: On Formal and Universal Unity
trans. by James F. Ross, 124 pp., $3.50

Cajetan: Commentary on St. Thomas Aquinas' On Being and Essence
trans. by Francis C. Wade, S.J. and Lottie Kendzierski, 356 pp., $6.50

Peter of Spain: Tractatus Syncategorematum and Selected Anonymous Treatises
trans. by Joseph P. Mullally, intro. by Joseph P. Mullally and Roland Houde
168 pp., $3.50

Desiderius Erasmus of Rotterdam: On Copia of Words and Ideas
trans. and intro. by Donald B. King and H. David Rix, 124 pp., $3.00

Aristotle: On Interpretation—Commentary by St. Thomas and Cajetan
trans. by Jean T. Oesterle, 288 pp., $6.50

St. Thomas Aquinas: On Charity   trans. by Lottie Kendzierski, 120 pp., $3.00

Hugh of St. Victor: Sololoquy on the Earnest Money of the Soul
trans. by Kevin Herbert, 48 pp., $1.50

John of St. Thomas: Outlines of Formal Logic
trans. by Francis C. Wade, S.J., 136 pp., $3.00

Giles of Rome: Theorems on Existence and Essence
trans. by Michael V. Murray, S.J., 128 pp., $2.50

Meditations of Guigo   trans. by John J. Jolin, S.J., 84 pp., $2.00

St. Thomas Aquinas: On Spiritual Creatures
trans. by Mary C. FitzPatrick, 135 pp., $2.00

Francis Suarez: On the Various Kinds of Distinctions
trans. by Cyril Vollert, S.J., 67 pp., $1.50

Pico Della Mirandola: Of Being and Unity trans. by Victor M. Hamm, 34 pp., $1.00

St. Augustine: Against the Academicians
trans. by Sr. Mary Patricia Garvey, R.S.M., 85 pp., $1.50